# LIFE ON THE MOVE

**LIFE ON THE MOVE**
Copyright © 2019 by Ann Gordon Bain
All rights reserved

Typesetting and Cover Design by
FormattingExperts.com

# LIFE ON THE MOVE

## Ann Gordon Bain

**I**

Home is a very important part of a person's life. It takes on even more significance when you don't have one.

During my childhood I was technically a refugee three times and changed schools fourteen times. Home was where my suitcase was. These disruptions affected the five members of our family quite differently.

For me, home became people more than a place. When I found myself at six years of age living in Oakland, California, with an elderly couple unrelated to me, I sorely missed my family, not a place. My mother was in a hospital somewhere and my brothers, aged nine and eleven, were staying alone in a hotel in San Francisco. My father was across an ocean.

Would I ever see my family again? I would have to soldier on and be a trooper. Our family highly valued dealing with things the way they were and not complaining, but it was difficult, especially for a small child.

Both my parents had childhood homes and my brothers and I visited them a few times, but they were not our home.

My father, Robert Gordon, was born in Dayton, Ohio, on January 1st, 1904, across the street from the Wright brothers' bicycle shop and only two weeks after their first powered flight. Dad was related to the brothers through Benjamin Van Cleve, a founder of Dayton.

When he was five years old and living in New Jersey, Benjamin witnessed the Battle of Monmouth during the American Revolution. As the British army neared his home, the men sought out the Patriot army to offer their services. They joined Colonel Morgan's riflemen and reconnoitered the British right flank. The women and children fled for safety to a pine woods nearby.

Young Benjamin snuck off to explore for himself but returned to the safety of his family when he heard British army bugles and knew the red coats were near. After the battle, the British retreated to Sandy Hook and the family returned to their home to find little more than a naked chimney. They saved a bed, a yearling heifer and a sow with a broken back. Benjamin's father's blacksmith's shop was burnt but his anvil remained. Over the next few years the British periodically returned for raids and his father continued to serve in the militia.

In 1785 Benjamin's family moved to western Pennsylvania. Four years later they moved again, down the Ohio River to the mouth of the Licking River where his father, John Van Cleve, registered lots in what became Cincinnati. In his journal, stored in the Dayton public library, Benjamin reported that on June 1, 1791, his father was working in one of his fields when Indians appeared. As John ran under a tree an Indian jumped down upon him, stabbing him five times and taking his scalp. When the men from adjoining lots reached him, John was already dead.

Dad's grandmother, Laura Andrews Poling, told a different version of this story. She said John's wife Catherine, in their cabin, heard the whooping, grabbed her gun, flung open the door and shot and killed the Indian as he ran. Benjamin Van Cleve was eighteen at the time of his father's death and determined to take the place of his father in providing for his mother and younger sisters. His mother remarried not long after her husband's death.

The family moved again to establish a new settlement, Dayton, where they thought they would be safer. But the Indian threat followed them. One evening Indians, under the influence of fire-water (alcohol), surrounded their cabin and demanded admission. The family removed one of the split logs from the puncheon floor and Benjamin's youngest sister, twelve-year-old Mary, crept through the small aperture. She ran for help from men at the local tavern and brought them back to her cabin. The Indians, faced with more opponents, dispersed.

Benjamin remained in Dayton becoming its first post-master, first school teacher and first clerk of the court. These stories of bygone days fascinated Dad, particularly those told by his grandmother Poling, Benjamin's granddaughter. Indians no longer threatened Dayton, but perhaps he might find his own adventures elsewhere.

When he was five, Dad's family moved to the outskirts of Dayton to Grandma Poling's farm. Her father had built the house of bricks he made himself, and given it to her as a wedding present along with a one-hundred-acre farm. Dad had an opportunity to listen to other family stories, including those about her two brothers who served in the Civil War.

One brother came hobbling down the road after the war, emaciated but alive. He had survived on little more than hardtack (hard bread). The other entered the service as a sur-geon in the 103rd army corps. He contracted pneumonia in Chattanooga and died in the hospital in Atlanta. Grandma Poling was proud of her family and their service. She added Civil War stories to the Indian stories that so intrigued Dad. He formed a strong bond with this grandmother. He rarely mentioned his Grandpa Poling, except to say he was a bit of a jokester. Dad didn't know how well his grandfather could read. Grandpa Poling often sat with the Bible in his lap, turn-ing two or three pages at a time.

Dad had two brothers, Bill four and a half years older, and Ed three years older, and a sister, Laura, three years younger. Dad and his father had dark, curly hair but his brother Ed and his sister Laura were blond as children. Everyone helped on the farm doing what he or she could. Dad, being the youngest boy, emptied the chamber pots and the slop pots for the pigs, an unpleasant task but not dangerous. Once a week it was his job to churn the cream from their milk into butter.

Neither Grandpa Poling nor Dad's father were physically able to do much of the heavy work on the farm. His older brothers, Bill and Ed, often had to perform jobs normally done by men. One spring Ed, about thirteen years old, was driving a team of horses hitched to a disc harrow across a field. A bee stung one of the horses and Ed lost control of them. He was thrown off his perch and struck the roller as he fell, tearing a gash in the side of his face. The doctor arrived hours later. Ed developed lockjaw (now called tetanus) and nearly died. He retained a severe facial scar the rest of his life.

Animals performed an integral role in their daily lives. In addition to cows, horses, chickens and pigs there was usually at least one dog and many cats. Once when Dad was walking his dog across a railroad trestle, a train suddenly appeared. He dropped down to hang off the bottom of the bridge and survived, but his dog did not.

Their animal friends were not always so unlucky. Sometimes when the barn teemed with cats, the boys would try to give them away or abandon them at a considerable distance from the farm, but the cats always returned. In desperation, one day they put a cat in a burlap bag with a rock, took it down to the river, and threw it in. The cat returned to the barn by milking time.

The family maintained a large vegetable garden which provided much of their food and needed constant tending by his mother and the younger children. One of Dad's tasks was to find the eggs (the chickens ranged freely) and gather the corn cobs for the kitchen stove. "Bob, Bob, the Corn Cob!" his brothers teased him derisively. The children were able to attend a one room school house about a quarter of a mile down a dirt road from the farm and across the Mad River from the Huffman Prairie. The teacher boarded in their home one quarter of each year as the Gordons formed one quarter of the students in the school.

After the Wright brothers' initial flights in Kitty Hawk, North Carolina, the brothers moved to the Huffman Prairie to further develop their planes. From the Gordon farm fields and his school Dad could see planes circling above the prairie. His father knew the brothers, so one day he took Dad over to the hangar to meet them. Dad distinctly remembered the incident because he was five and trying hard to shake hands correctly and to perform formal introductions. The brothers continued to operate a flying school there from 1910 to 1916. One of their students was Henry "Hap" Arnold who later commanded the US Army Air Corps in WWII and became the first commander of the US Air Force.

Dad's father, Edwin Reed Gordon, suffered from either a club foot or paralysis from polio. The family never discussed his condition, so Dad never knew the source of the problem. His family was warm but reserved. His father had attended high school for three years and then took night courses at a business college. There he learned the skills necessary to secure him a job as a bookkeeper in a last factory (wooden forms for shoes).

In 1914 he secured a new job at a last factory in Rochester, New York, and the family moved there. Dad's mother, Jeanette Poling Gordon, had graduated from high school and strongly wanted her children to do the same. In Rochester his father would have a better job and the children would have better schools.

The grandparents back in Dayton could not do all the farm work themselves. A tenant farmer was engaged to work the land on shares. The grandparents' little income now came from milk and egg sales and their share of the tenant's meager profits. Every summer one or two of the Gordon children would return to Dayton to help their grandparents with farm chores. These trips to and from Dayton via an uncle in Cleveland were the first of several small trips Dad took in his youth. Once, instead of taking a train from Cleveland to Rochester, he took a lake boat to Buffalo and made a side trip to Niagara Falls. Eventually his grandparents left the Dayton farm and moved in with his family in a larger house in Rochester and the trips ceased.

When Dad was fourteen he, and only a third of his class, continued on to high school. He then received an allowance of twenty-five cents per week, but he needed five cents a day for milk at school. It would be nice to have a little extra cash to pay for a streetcar ride in bad weather or an occasional chocolate. His solution was to start his own small business buying magazines in town and reselling them house to house in his neighborhood for a small profit.

Soon he also became involved in peddling the high school paper. The high school consisted of a girls' side and a boys' side—the boys sold the paper on the girls' side and vice versa. Although quite shy, he found one way to meet girls was to peddle the papers. He also wanted to be a reporter but the ability to type was required. The school only offered typing classes to girls. He learned it was possible to rent a typewriter for one month so he saved up enough money, borrowed a book on typing from the library, taught himself to type and became a school reporter.

In June 1920, though just sixteen, he was old enough to get an adult job and began work during the summer in a fireworks factory. He worked alone in a small brick building in a line of similar buildings. It was easy work but the first day he realized how dangerous it was. The buildings were constructed so that, if there were an explosion, the blast would explode out, thus destroying only one building and killing only one person. He didn't want to be the one person. He needed money, but not at the cost of his life. He quit and took a safer job packing peaches and cherries for canning.

As a young boy, he had watched the Civil War veterans march by in parades and had listened to stories from Grandma Poling about her brothers in the war. So one summer, after he earned money working in a local drugstore, he and a high school buddy decided to go to the Citizen's Military Training Camp in Plattsburgh, New York. The army gave him money for train fare to and from Plattsburgh. On the way home, instead of taking a train, he took a Great Lakes steam boat from Montreal up the St. Lawrence River and Lake Erie to Rochester. His bunk mate had a trunk with stickers from London, Bombay and Cairo. Was it possible he could ever go to those places?

In the fall of his senior year he came down with diphtheria, a life-threatening disease in those days. He was quarantined and lost a lot of school time. When he was able to return, the principal suggested he drop back a half-grade so that he could graduate in June rather than in January-it would be a better time to enter college. College? No one had ever mentioned he might go to college.

He became Editor-in-Chief of the yearbook in his senior year and chose half his staff from the girls' side of the school. He knew many of them from his experience selling papers there, but the new job meant closer contact. He enjoyed a few dates with some of them but felt awkward and shabbily dressed. Fortunately, some of his male friends filled him in on etiquette. A few of them were going on to college after graduation and seemed so much more sophisticated than he was.

Dad had no money for college. His high school Latin teacher encouraged him to become a Latin professor but he would have to have a college degree. His parents felt they put the three boys through high school and now it was their sister Laura's turn. He would be on his own after high school. Following a short spell in the US Army tank corps during World War I, his brother Bill worked as a postman. His brother Ed had also served in the army in WWI. Ed suggested Dad go to the University of Rochester and at least inquire about what it would take to attend there. He did, but the tuition fee of $200 ended that possibility. There was no way he could come up with $200.

One day Principal Willcox took him aside.

"What are your plans for next year?"

"I will be looking for a job," Dad said.

"Did you consider going to college?" he asked.

"Yes. I went to the University of Rochester and they said it would cost $200 per year to attend. I don't have the money."

"Let me see if I can help," he replied. "Go speak to the Freshman Dean with a recommendation from me and we'll see what he can do."

Dad returned and spoke to the Freshman Dean. To his amazement, the college offered him a $100 a year scholarship if he maintained an 80 average. He considered how he might earn the balance. His bubble burst when his mother asked how he would pay for his room and board. She pointed out she couldn't give him something she had not given his brothers. After graduation, he would owe her $2 per week if he lived at home.

He didn't remember his high school graduation (he was already at work behind an ice cream counter) but he graduated second in his class. In July he received a letter from the Board of Education awarding him a Monroe County Scholarship worth a hundred dollars at any college in the state! Tuition problem solved, in August he attended the coastal artillery camp in New Jersey, taking extra time traveling down and back to see the sites at army expense. He was going to college!

Only two percent of high school graduates continued their education on to college. Principal Willcox told him college functioned like an insurance policy—if he got a bachelor's degree he could always get a job—which is the way Dad viewed it. It would be necessary to maintain an eighty average in an era when a C or seventy-five was the real average, but he thought himself capable of handling the work.

He signed up for the football team (never having played football), the school paper and the only fraternity which invited him. Dad was fairly tall, thin and well-coordinated. He was assigned to play center on the football team his first year. There were no offensive and defensive teams—everyone played continuously. Injuries occurred frequently as players wore little protection. His father, never able to participate in sports due to his limp, came to all Dad's games and sat on a nearby hillside as he could not afford the cost of a ticket. From this vantage point he watched the game but could not see the scoreboard, so Dad gave him the results when the game was over.

When the football season finished, Dad took his reporting role more seriously. He secured a part-time job as a stringer for the Rochester Democrat and Chronicle, the city newspaper, which paid him by the inch for anything of his they published. He covered all college news not related to sports as that was already the domain of another student reporter. This broad assignment gave him access to the college president, faculty and deans-important contacts he could use later. He continued his athletic activity with basketball in the winter and track in the spring.

His first fraternity membership only lasted a few days as he quickly realized these young men had different goals than he did. Later, after he became active in the newspaper, he joined a different fraternity whose members included several of the reporters on the college paper. The fraternity cost additional money, so he took another job tutoring Latin to two young girls from a wealthy family. They needed Latin to enter a New England preparatory school. The job would provide him experience doing what he planned to do after college, teach Latin. In the spring the family hired him as a full-time chauffeur and Latin instructor if he would accompany them to Nantucket for the summer. He accepted-it would give him another chance to travel.

As chauffeur, he drove their Willy's St. Clair sedan from Rochester to Nantucket and wore a chauffeur's uniform. Roads were one or two lanes, often unpaved and in poor condition. Flats were common. One of his jobs was to fix flat tires as they occurred. In New Bedford he found time to visit the whaling museum before driving the Willy's onto the car ferry which took them to Nantucket.

The family's house on the bluffs overlooking the sound accommodated their family of five, eight live-in servants and guests. This job exposed Dad to people of a much higher financial status than he had previously encountered, and he found wealthy people were not unlike himself. He lived in a boarding house in town with vacationers and other employees, many of whom worked as teachers the rest of the year. He met a Latin professor from a college in Ohio and asked questions about his future career.

His sophomore year brought a gradual change in direction. His Latin, Greek and French courses seemed less appealing and unrelated to real life. In contrast, his history professor, Dr. Packard, had been in Siberia with the U.S. Army after World War I. His subjects appeared much more exciting than those of a Latin professor. Dad considered shifting his major to history with the goal of possibly becoming a history professor. The childhood stories of Grandma Poling had whetted his taste for tales of adventure.

In Nantucket for a second summer he no longer needed to teach the girls Latin as they now studied Latin in their boarding schools. He enjoyed more free time and decided to go into the lobster business with another summer employee, Jimmy Gray. They bought a lobster trap and rented a rowboat. The first day they rowed out, set the trap, marked its location, and rowed back. The next day they rowed out to the trap and found it untouched. When they headed back they ran into trouble. Dad described what happened in his book *Something Worthwhile*[*]:

> *The hour was late, and the tide had turned. We made slow progress as the night darkened. Inside the break-water the tide was even stronger, and the lights of the distant town seemed as heaven. Suddenly, one of my two oarlocks came out and fell into the water; we had only three useful oars! Now we went backwards with the tide, and in desperation I took the laces out of my shoes, tied the oar to the oarlock and pulled carefully away. It was ten at night when we reached the dock and thus ended our adventure in the lobster business.*

Jimmy Gray left after a month and then the Latin professor from Ohio returned. He tried to teach Dad to sing in Latin, but Dad maintained he was tone deaf and could barely sing in English. Eventually the professor suggested Dad share his bed. Their relationship ended as did any remaining interest Dad had in Latin.

In his junior year Dad moved to second string quarterback. He liked the challenge but knew he would not make varsity quarterback in his senior year if he enjoyed another soft summer on Nantucket. He decided to look for a construction job. At that time, one didn't look for work until he was ready to start. One of his classmates completed his exams earlier than Dad and took a job helping build the

---

[*] Gordon, Robert M. *Something Worthwhile, Recollections of R.M. Gordon, Sr.* 1980

Sibley Tower in Rochester. His first day at work his friend stepped on a loose plank and fell, breaking his leg. Dad got the vacant job.

The work was dangerous and physically demanding. One day a laborer looked down a temporary elevator shaft for the cement bucket. It dropped from above and cut off his head. You not only had to be careful of what you did but also you had to watch out for another person's mistake. Once a red-hot rivet landed beside him, probably dropped by a riveter somewhere in the steel above him. No one wore hard hats, so it might have killed him. It was said one life was lost for every ten floors of construction. By the time the top floor was completed he had learned to routinely walk eight-inch girders, always with care. He wrote of his final task on the site:

> It was I who laid the final plaster block on the ceiling of the thirteenth floor. This required standing on a trestle with a plank sticking out over the street while fitting the pins at each end of the 25-lb. block into steel loops imbedded in the cement of the underside of the roof above. I glanced at the 250-lb colored man holding the other end of the plank and walked out over the street carrying the block, turned, hoisted it and fitted the four pins into their small loops.

With the roof finished on the Sibley building, he was no longer needed. He then found a job laying curbstones in a new sub-division. This meant digging with pick and shovel and involved thirty men, all of whom spoke Italian except Dad.

In the fall he returned in superb shape for football practice and made varsity quarterback and captain. He claimed he was only an average quarterback but reportedly made an excellent flying tackle. Not many opponents got past him. He felt he was good at reading the opponent's plays, an important ability for a quarterback when they made their own calls. He was elected president of his fraternity and of the senior class. At the same time he fell in love with a co-ed who was planning to become a nurse—until she broke up with him to date another classmate. In the spring of his senior year he had a few double dates with Milly Gleichauf (later my Mom) who had broken up with her boyfriend. She told Dad she thought it would be fun to "go out with a brain for a change," and he had just been elected to Phi Beta Kappa.

He had switched from Latin to history because he preferred to study a subject with action, not a dead language. Now he realized history, although studying events and people rather than language, was still not dynamic enough for him. He wanted to be the person who did things, not the person who wrote about what others had done. His professors suggested he earn a master's degree in political economy, a field which offered opportunities in both academia and business. The University offered him a teaching assistant position while he worked for the degree and he accepted.

After college graduation he enjoyed another summer in Nantucket with the same wealthy family as he no longer had to worry about conditioning for football. He admired the life they led and aspired for it for himself. He realized being a professor of almost anything would not be an entry into the Nantucket life style or the traveling he so much enjoyed. At the end of the summer he rented an old Ford roadster for $2 per week and toured New England with a friend. Driving from Boston to Amherst they had thirteen flat tires in one day. They spent a lot of time patching tires, but Dad loved it anyway.

Back at the University of Rochester in graduate school he chose George Aldridge, Republican boss of the city of Rochester in the days of George Eastman, as his thesis topic. The thesis was so good he received an interview to discuss it with Frank Gannett, founder of Gannett Newspapers. He had little time for social life that year as he focused more on his career. Travel was his dream, and he saw a professor's life as geographically limited and only modestly remunerative but he was not sure what path to follow.

Dad visited the Eastman Kodak office in Rochester three separate times to apply for a job in their Export department but failed to receive an offer. Eventually he found a job in Cine-Kodak, a department formed to develop the educational movie business. It was not travel, but it was in a real business and with Kodak. Maybe someday…

His job involved answering letters from customers about home movie services. It was routine and boring. After working about four months, his boss called him into his office. From *Something Worthwhile*:

> *"Did you write this letter to Mr. (X)?" the boss demanded as I entered his office. He held up the carbon copy of the letter where I could see my name on it.*
>
> *"Yes, Sir," I said meekly, not knowing what to expect.*
>
> *"It says here that we have not received his film and, let me quote, 'We'll gladly clean and copy your film as soon as it arrives. We can assure you of prompt and satisfactory service.'" The boss tried to control his temper, looked at me with murder in his eyes, and continued, "Don't you know that Mr. X was here ten days ago and handed the film to me personally?"*
>
> *The boss got to his feet, waved my letter in the air and couldn't find words until he almost shouted in my ear, "Do you want to ruin our business? Do you call this giving prompt and satisfactory service? Did you ever look for his film? Or were you too tired to get up from your chair? What have you got to say for yourself?"*
>
> *He was fired. He went back to his desk to clean out his things.*

A co-worker, Malcom MacBride, asked him what he was doing.

"I'm fired. I'm going home," I answered softly.

"You're fired! What for?" he demanded.

"I wrote a customer that we had not received his film," I said, "when actually he had delivered it to the boss in person ten days ago..."

"What was the customer's name?" Mac asked.

"Mr. X." I almost whispered the evil word. "Two 400-foot reels of film."

"Sit down and wait a minute," he commanded. I sank unresisting into my chair and was glad it had arms.

In a moment Mac was back and said, "Here's the film. The boss gave it to me one day when you were out and said he'd give me the instructions later. I never got the instructions, so I put the film in my desk."

Together they took the film to the boss who, after reprimanding them for not communicating with each other, sent them both back to their desks. Soon afterwards Dad was transferred to the Export Department where he had originally tried to find work. He never learned if there was any connection to the lost film incident.

Six months after joining the Export Department he was asked if he would like to go overseas. He enthusiastically accepted and began rotating through an extensive training program. Then he was instructed to be prepared to depart for the Philippines in two weeks. He would be leaving home for at least three years and possibly forever, but he was more than ready to go. Milly Gleichauf was working on the outskirts of Rochester at the time, preparing to move to New York City, but she came to Rochester to say goodbye. They did not expect to see each other again.

Dad enjoyed the train trip across the continent, especially listening to the clatter of the train wheels as they crossed switches taking him further and further into the unknown. It felt as if he were really going somewhere. There were no trans Pacific air flights in the 1920s, so in San Francisco he boarded the S.S. President Monroe. Travel was leisurely by steamer and he met Kodak employees at each port, including Honolulu, Yokohama, Kobe, Shanghai and Hong Kong. There was always a willing Kodak guide to show him the sights. He landed in Manila exactly one month after he had left Rochester, in April 1929. He had found his occupation, but had he found adventure?

* * *

After a brief stint living in the Manila YMCA, Dad moved into a rental house with three other bachelors. They had four servants—a cook, a houseboy and two laundresses. In the tropics, one wore a fresh white linen suit daily, which required a great deal of washing for four men. A Spanish family had trained the cook before the American seizure of the Philippines. He did not speak English and knew little of American preferences. The bachelors noticed there was never pie for dessert, so they asked the houseboy to ask the cook to make one. Shortly thereafter, they were served a delicious lemon meringue pie—upside down. Nowhere did the recipe indicate what the final arrangement should be.

Dad always attempted to learn the language of the places where he lived but he constantly struggled with its spoken form. He claimed he was tone deaf which would explain his poor singing as well as his difficulty with tonal languages. In the Philippines he made several business trips out of Manila to assess the needs of dealers in other places. His No. 1 Filipino, Mr. Capili, would accompany him. As a youth under the Spanish, Mr. Capili had been trained as a priest and learned Spanish and Latin as well as his native Tagalog. Now, working with Americans, he also spoke English. Dad could sing "Adeste Fideles" in Latin with him, but Mr. Capili knew all the verses, not just one. Once a Belgian priest stopped in the Manila office and wanted to buy a movie camera but needed operating instructions. Dad's French was too rudimentary for this task, but Mr. Capili was able to explain the camera's operation-in Latin.

The Americans took great care of their health in the Philippines because they were exposed to many tropical diseases for which they had little immunity. Each man slept under his own mosquito net for protection from the myriad insects. Geckos (small lizards) were permitted in the house because they ate the mosquitos. Dad caught dengue fever, commonly called *break-bone fever* because one ached inside as if your bones had been broken. One had to be careful of fresh vegetables due to dysentery (one of their employees died of it) and they did not go barefoot due to ringworm and other contagious diseases. They took shots every six months for cholera and drank quinine water with their gin to stave off malaria (or so they told themselves).

Dad gave considerable thought to the geopolitical situation. Prior to the Spanish-American War it had been assumed colonies existed for the benefit of the mother country. A debate in Congress ensued after the war with some suggesting the Philippines be developed for the benefit of the Filipinos, not the Americans. President McKinley argued against traditional colonialism in favor of encouraging future independence for *our little brown brothers*, a term which aided the Filipinos at the time but later was considered racist.

Most of Dad's activity outside of work consisted of time at the Polo Club playing tennis, softball, or swimming. There was a nine-hole golf course which had been built within the moat surrounding the old Spanish walled city of Manila. During siesta time (a tropical two-hour break in the afternoon) he would almost run with his friends from hole to deserted hole to get in a quick round. On Sunday afternoons the men dressed in their best and attended tea dances at the club. There were few girls available, most of them daughters of military men. The competition was fierce and Dad felt he often ended up on the short end.

When he earned a ten-day vacation, Dad drove up into the mountains of northern Luzon with his friend Mac McGrath. Head hunting was still practiced in the area although it was illegal. The following is an excerpt from Dad's book *Something Worthwhile*:

> *Turning west into the mountains near Banaue, my Ford got stuck in the mud as we forded a small stream. It was a new road, and there were no bridges. Despite our efforts Mac and I were stranded. Suddenly I saw two white-streaked faces peering at me through a bush. I stopped shoving the car, and Mac followed my gaze.*
>
> *"Hello!" I said.*
>
> *There was no answer, but two small very black men came forward. They wore only G-strings, and each carried a spear and a shield.*
>
> *"Come here," I demanded although I knew they could speak no English. "Push!" I waved them closer and demonstrated my words by pushing on the car. Without hesitation they laid down their spears and shields and joined me in the shallow water while Mac drove. In a moment the car was on high ground, and the two jumped up and down with glee. From the glove compartment I got two boxes of matches and gave one to each. They seemed pleased but stayed nearby while we washed and prepared to move on.*
>
> *"Banaue?" one said and pointed down the trail. I got the idea, opened the rumble seat, and signalled them to*

*get in. Picking up their weapons they climbed in, spears sticking out as from a man-of-war.*

*As we approached Banaue, I stopped the car to admire the view of the valley below. Suddenly, our guests in the open seat behind us shouted something, banged on the car, and pushed forward with their hands, signalling us to move on. When they pointed overhead, I saw a large boa constrictor on the limb of a tree stretching out over our heads. At a movie studio I had once seen a similar snake crush, kill and swallow whole a young pig, and I knew in hunger this one might drop on us. To hell with the view, we drove on.*

Clearly he had found an adventurous life, but was that all he wanted?

## II

My mother, Mildred Gleichauf (Milly), was born in Rochester, New York, on June 21st, 1905. Her father, Ed, was the second son of John Gleichauf who had immigrated from Germany in 1854 and established a successful grocery store in Rochester. At eleven or twelve, Ed hid his books and refused to return to school.

He began work in the family business where he became the butcher and fix-it man. Although he had little formal education, he came up with many practical ideas. To preserve food longer, he invented a walk-in refrigeration unit for the store with an escape hatch in case someone was caught inside. He built it himself and used it to freeze strawberries for Christmas and other occasions. At his suggestion, the store bought and maintained a delivery car when they became available. Maintenance of the vehicles was his responsibility. In those days cars frequently had flat tires, so he developed a tubeless tire. If a nail punctured it, the hole sealed itself as one withdrew the nail. He applied for a patent, but he lacked business acumen, and nothing came of his inventions.

Ed fell in love with a perky young cashier who worked in the grocery store, Elizabeth Crawford (Lizzie). Her forbearers were Scotch/Irish and dreadfully poor. They lived next to the railroad tracks in Dunkirk, New York, and many died young of tuberculosis. Lizzie was the first member of her family to break out of grinding poverty. Her mother passed away at age twenty-five, shortly after the birth of twins, one of whom died as an infant. Their grandmother, although she was still raising some of her own children, took in Lizzie and the surviving twin, Matie.

Lizzie left Dunkirk as soon as she was old enough and took office jobs in Rochester. Then she began working as a cashier in the Gleichauf grocery store and married the boss's son. Soon she had a one-carat diamond ring, a house and a buggy. She was ambitious, hard-working and extremely serious, unlike her sister Matie. Mom wrote this story of Matie in her childhood recollections:

> *She was invited to a party in Dunkirk and she didn't have anything to wear. She scrounged around and got all the colored bits of ribbon and cloth she could find. It was the era of patchwork quilts and people kept and reused everything. She made them into bows and sewed them all over her petticoat and wowed the party!*
>
> *As soon as Lizzie could after her marriage, she brought Aunt Matie to live with them.*

Ed and Lizzie had four children: twins Ray and Ralph, Crawford and Milly. Ed wanted his twin sons to work with him in the store, but Lizzie insisted they go to college and they did—the University of Michigan. Crawford was mentally handicapped. Mom never knew exactly what the problem was. Perhaps he had what we now diagnose as autism. He went to school and learned to read and write. Lizzie expected Mom to stay in Rochester and care for Crawford during his lifetime, a responsibility Mom would not assume. She reported she learned about sex while caring for this older brother. She couldn't decide how to tell her parents of the abuse, but she knew she would leave home as soon as she could.

When the family finances became worse and the grocery business declined, her parents became so estranged they seldom spoke to each other. Ed would say "Tell your mother…" and Lizzie would reply "Tell your father…" Mom became the interpreter. Everything about her family seemed gloomy. Even the food was depressing—heavy German meals of meat and potatoes when Mom wanted to eat fresh salads. From *Milly*[*]:

> *One Sunday while making a salad I needed a Bermuda onion. It was cold and dark in the basement of our house, and I picked up a tulip bulb instead of an onion. Cutting it into the salad, I didn't cry, noticed my mistake, got an onion and cut it into the salad, too.*
>
> *After dinner I laughed and told my family. There was a dead silence, then a groan from Father, and Crawford ran to the bathroom and vomited. Soon they were all sick. Just then Ernie came to take me some place, and he suggested I call a doctor. When I told the doctor what I had done, he asked to see the tulip bulbs, then announced tulip bulbs wouldn't hurt anybody. Immediately they all got better.*

Mom was tall for her era and full grown in the eighth grade. She considered herself plain looking but others described her as pretty. With brown hair, hazel eyes and a pug nose, she attracted attention and was popular. She earned the lead in her high school play. Opening night a big fire broke out in Rochester and everyone left the play to see the fire. So much for her moment in the spotlight.

Some people know how to get things done, and Mom was one of them. Negotiation was often her strategy. She told this story about her father in the *Gordon Genealogies*[**]:

---

[*] Gordon, Robert M. *Milly, A Biography.* 1979
[**] Gordon, Bruce E. *The Gordon Genealogies. Robert, Bruce and Ann Gordon Families.* 1990

*I never saw Ed get angry. The only time I can remember him correcting me was to tell me to go clean my teeth and never be seen again without them clean. Then when I started playing tennis, he demanded I wear black stockings—he didn't want to see bare legs. I agreed, if he would stop putting his napkin into his collar (as was the German custom), it embarrassed me. He agreed, and we both kept our word.*

Although it was not a happy household, Mom said she admired some of her mother's characteristics, many of which she too possessed. Lizzie always thought things could be better. The grocery business serviced the mansions on East Avenue and the elegant lifestyle of those homes fueled Lizzie's ambition. She collected her friends carefully and kept them for life. She set an elegant table. She was always open to the newest thing and read widely. She dressed with care but considered love of color and clothes sinful. On this matter, mother and daughter disagreed.

In high school Mom was infatuated by Wink, an excellent athlete but a Catholic. Her father objected vehemently to Wink's religion and when Wink went away to college they gradually separated. Mom's twin brothers, twelve years older, had graduated from college and she assumed she would too. She applied to and was accepted at the University of Rochester. At the end of her sophomore year she received a grant to travel west on a geological project. The trip broke whatever hold her family had on her. She assuaged her unhappiness both at home and in her love life by over-eating and gained weight. She skipped classes and wanted out but did not know how. The Dean settled it for her by notifying her she did not have enough credits to graduate with her class.

Since she was now leaving the University she needed to get a job to support herself when she left home. She took a six-week secretarial course at the Rochester Business Institute and accepted employment in the Brockport library outside Rochester. The work was routine, boring and isolating. Why not leave for the big city? She located a job in New York at Columbia Dental College. Her boss there had just returned from two years in China with the Rockefeller Foundation and she wondered if somehow she might travel there.

Living in New York City was expensive, so it took time for her to save up enough money to travel to Europe with her friend Esther Wood. Esther returned home at the end of their European trip in order to marry her beau. Mom had no such attachment and determined to work her way around the world alone. She cashed in her return ticket to New York and bought a one-way ticket on a steamer bound for Manila and Shanghai. Single educated Western women were scarce in the Orient and on the ship heading east she had several marriage proposals. One came from a plantation manager in Malaya and another from a banker in Singapore. She turned down both of them. Mom even received a proposal from a man she had known for six hours!

When the ship stopped in Manila, she reconnected with Dad. They had kept in touch by letters over the years and he was delighted when Mom showed up in Manila for two weeks. He monopolized her time completely, and she loved it. They lunched on the veranda of the Manila Hotel and watched the ships in the harbor. They swam at the Polo club and dined and danced there almost nightly. One weekend they took a native canoe up the Pagsanjan River to the water falls. They toured shops and the walled city but mostly they talked and talked. He began to think about the idea of marriage—was he ready? She wasn't—she continued on to Shanghai.

Mom arrived in Shanghai with only twenty dollars. Her first job was to find a place to stay, and she headed directly to the Y.W.C.A. where she secured a room on credit. They told her about an automotive agency which wanted a secretary and she took the job. She was safe until payday, but on a financial diet. She soon found she had a dinner date almost every evening paid for by some Western bachelor.

When she mentioned at the Y she wanted to go on to Beijing, they suggested she get in touch with the Beijing Union Medical College run by the Rockefeller Foundation. The Foundation's secretary had eloped with a Marine and the Beijing job was available if she would come for an interview. One of their doctors was in Shanghai and arranged to see her the next day. She was promptly hired, given US$100 for passage to Beijing, and urged to take the first ship available. The Shanghai newspaper listed a German freighter leaving in an hour for Tientsin, the port of Beijing. Could she make it? She rushed off to try to catch the ship. The following description of the trip, from Mom's point of view, is from Dad's book *Milly*:

*As I walked up the gangplank, there was no one to be seen. I couldn't imagine why I was alone, but I went below to find the Purser and to buy a ticket. All I found was a Chinese servant who spoke no English but assumed I wanted a cabin. He showed me to a comfortable room, and I moved in…*

*Moments later bells rang, the ship's engines started up, and we were on our way. With my purse under my arm I went on deck to see the sights as we moved down the Whangpoo River. The little sampans we passed seemed to dance as they rocked in the wake of our ship, and the green rice fields on shore slid silently by.*

*Still it seemed there was no one on board. I was on a phantom ship outbound to the China Sea! Finally, I noticed a short, slim and well-dressed Oriental gentleman watching me from behind a ship's winch. My heart jumped. When he realized I had seen him, he came forward. He'd have been handsome if I hadn't thought him so mysterious.*

*"What are you doing here?" he demanded brusquely but in perfect English—the King's English, that is.*

*"I'm going to Peking and I want to buy a ticket," I said, assuming he was a ship's officer.*

*"Not on this ship," he thundered. I was surprised so little a man could muster such vehemence.*

*"The Shanghai newspaper reported that this ship is going to Tientsin," I said. "Isn't that right?"*

*"That's right, but you're not," he said with a clipped British accent as his temper mounted. "There are no females on this ship, and there never will be!" He almost shouted at me as if the force of his words would make me disappear. It was my sex that aroused his ire. "I can't very well get off," I reasoned, looking over the ship's rail at the muddy waters gliding by.*

*"We'll see about that!" he declared grimly, his dark Oriental eyes afire with determination. "Follow me," he ordered. "We'll go see the Captain about this."*

*Up on the ship's bridge all China seemed spread before us, and our watery ribbon twisted across the flat countryside as if to delay our escape. The heavy-set Captain bowed as we entered the pilot house.*

*"Your Highness?" he asked with a German accent.*

*"This female must be sent back to Shanghai at once!" the little man demanded. He scarcely came to my shoulder, but he spoke with authority, and I waited with amusement to learn how these foreigners would decide my fate.*

*The Captain hesitated. "Your Highness," he asked diffidently. "How are we to do that?" He glanced out the windows at the rice fields we could almost touch. "We cannot turn around here, and we cannot delay our Charter."*

The dark and sallow face of my antagonist suddenly flushed with new anger. I was finding the inscrutable Oriental not so mysterious as fascinating. The gentleman's black, shiny hair was smoothly combed and as neat as his pin-striped suit and shining black shoes. He might have been straight from the shop of a London tailor, and he was obviously not accustomed to being crossed. He vented his anger on me.

"Why do you do this to me?" he demanded.

"Your Highness," I bowed, taking my cue from the Captain. "I am sorry if I have somehow inconvenienced you. I am an American on my way to Peking to take a job at the Peking Union Medical College. There is no other ship going to Tientsin at this time."

His Highness turned to the windows to look out ahead of us and idly to watch a channel buoy slip easily by. Silently we waited. A gray-haired and even smaller Asian gentleman appeared in the doorway and also waited. Slowly his Highness confronted me.

"You should know that I am Prince Purachatra of Siam. My brother is the King, and I am heading a trade delegation to China. This ship is under lease to His Majesty's Government for this mission. Your presence is most embarrassing."

"Your Highness" I told him. "I apologize for my ignorance. The shipping report said nothing about that. I want to pay for my ticket."

The Prince curiously recoiled as if I had struck him. Apparently he had assumed everyone knew about his mission. Again, since I offered to pay for my ticket, I couldn't be a stowaway. The older man in the doorway now came fully in, bowed to the Prince and spoke in a language I did not understand. After an interchange His Highness asked me, "Are you a doctor or a nurse?"

27

"No, Your Highness" I said. "I am to be a secretary to Dr. Gee. My last job was as a medical secretary at Columbia University in New York City, but I wanted to see the world."

"You American women are impossible," he exploded, then turned back to his secretary, obviously to discuss my case further. Ignoring me, the Prince finally turned to the Captain, stretched to his noble highest and said to the Captain as if I were not there, "If the Captain of this ship were to make no mention of this female in his ship's log, it would really not make sense to turn around." He gazed ahead as we entered the seemingly borderless Yangtze River.

After a moment the big German bowed and said, "Your Highness, by the terms of my Charter no females are allowed on this ship. Any word of it and my career would be ruined."

There was a long silence until I noticed the Prince glance towards the door as if to leave, so I spoke up. "How much is my ticket?" and I opened my purse.

The Prince stopped and turned to me scornfully, "If you are not here," he said, "how can you pay for your ticket?" Without waiting for an answer, he stalked out, calling over his shoulder, "Dinner is at eight."

Quietly I asked, "Does one dress for dinner?"

"Naturally" he dryly informed me as he disappeared out the door followed by his secretary. I was glad then that I had a long strapless dinner dress with me, but later I learned that bare neck and shoulders were con- sidered sexy by Asian men. No wonder the Prince had trouble believing that I was not a Shanghai prostitute! I sat with him and his secretary at the Captain's table at dinner, and during the next three days I learned that His Highness was a graduate of Cambridge University in

*England. He asked me many questions about Columbia University, Women's Rights in America, why I wanted to see the world, and other things. He was polite, circumspect and cold, and I never saw him except at table.*

*I was surprised therefore when the Prince asked me to join him during the official reception scheduled for our arrival in Tientsin. One of his photographers later sent me a photo of the Prince and me driving through the streets of Tientsin in an open touring car. I remember bowing happily to cheering crowds on right and left. I'm sure they thought I was his mistress. As the parade ended, the Prince dropped me, my one suitcase and my portable typewriter—all my worldly goods and possessions—at the railway station in Tientsin.*

Mom stood at the station a little bewildered and afraid. She was alone in a sea of coolies, all of whom wanted to carry her bag and typewriter. As soon as she chose two, they chased off the others, and took her to the ticket counter where she purchased a ticket with only one word—Beijing. Moments later a European gentleman tipped his hat and offered his assistance. She noticed there always seemed to be an English-speaking person willing to help a single young woman—and often he was Chinese.

The novelty of life in Beijing fascinated her. The stores were grouped by type on streets whose names indicated what they contained. If you wanted to buy jade, you went to Jade Street and so forth. She soon learned to bargain for everything. She took a rickshaw to work daily and realized the same rickshaw driver was outside her door every morning. He kept the other rickshaw boys away and seemed to own her.

At first, she stayed in the home of a Chinese doctor from the Medical School. One day she overhead the doctor and a friend discussing the unfairness of the Medical College by paying their American doctors in American money at much higher levels than the Chinese staff in Chinese money. They talked of a strike and she feared for her safety. As soon as possible she teamed up with a group of five American gals to rent their own household and hire their own servants.

Mom became a close friend of Eleanor Breed who was working her own way westward around the world. They would come up with an idea and soon other young women like themselves would join them. Once they hired Mongolian ponies and rode out to the Western Hills outside Beijing where they spent the night in sleeping bags in the courtyard of an old temple. They decided to hike around the entire city wall of Beijing, a total of fourteen miles, but only two of them made the entire circuit—naturally Mom and Eleanor. The wall was later demolished to create a highway around the inner city and today only one tower remains. When they went to the Ming tombs, Mom climbed up into the arms of a huge Mandarin statue. She posed for a picture pretending to blow his nose with a handkerchief—but she slipped and fell, spraining her ankle.

I had my picture taken at the same statue many years later and so did my daughter and her cousin—a tradition which we hope to continue in future generations. One noticeable thing about each picture is the surroundings. In Mom's picture there are no trees at all because they had all been cut down for firewood. In my picture there are some small trees as they were protected by the government. In Jean's picture there are lots of large trees and barricades around the statues to prevent people from climbing on them.

When Mom took a visiting friend, Norma, around Beijing shopping, all the merchants overcharged the visitor.

"Norma," Mom said, "you are paying about twice what your purchases are worth. Let me help you bargain."

Norma wanted no coaching and insisted on doing it her way. Mom's rickshaw driver noticed what Norma was paying. The next day he approached Milly.

"We go backee now—get um *cum sha*." (pidgin English for kickback), he said.

She settled into his rickshaw and was taken to each of the stores where Norma had made purchases.

"You wait-ee here," he instructed Mom.

The driver soon returned with *cum sha* for her from the store owner and presumably one for himself. This scenario was repeated at each store where Norma had purchased something.

As with the doctors, she soon found there were two pay scales in Beijing. Those secretaries hired in the US were paid in American dollars while those hired in China were paid in Chinese yuan, worth considerably less. Although she loved her time in Beijing, after a year she decided to return to America, be rehired in New York City, and then return to China on a higher pay scale. To finance the trip, she came up with a scheme to buy fur lined Mandarin jackets and then sell them in Rochester. She borrowed US$300 from her uncle George Gleichauf and $100 from her father to pay for her transportation, put the jackets in a trunk with other salable items, and sent them to Rochester. She wrote a letter to Dad telling him of her plans.

She traveled by train through Manchuria and Korea, and became debilitated with a bad case of dysentery. Fortunately, in Pusan the Japanese Tourist Bureau took her in charge and managed to get her to Tokyo where a junior secretary in the American embassy nursed her back to health. The sea voyage from Yokohama to Vancouver was rough, accompanied by severe seasickness. In Rochester she found her family impossible, so she sold the jackets as expeditiously as possible (she kept one which I still have) and hurried off to New York City. There she was rehired for China. On the bulletin board at the International House in New York she saw the Japanese ambassador in Washington was looking for someone to escort his young son back to Tokyo. Mom took the job to cover the cost of her transportation back to Beijing and began preparing for her return.

Mom felt that the year in Beijing was the greatest learning year of her life. It shook up her Rochester attitudes towards religion, race, social mores and ambition. She had experienced excitement, thrills and generosity. Was she missing anything?

# III

Dad was completing his three-year stint in the Philippines when he received orders from Kodak headquarters transferring him from Manila to Santiago, Chile. He was instructed to proceed there via the home office in Rochester. Several of his bachelor friends in Manila had recently married and appeared to be happy. Perhaps time was passing him by. He wanted a family and, from his experiences trying to get dates in Manila, he realized how difficult it was to find women willing to live the life of adventure he already loved. From her regular letters, he knew Mom was temporarily back in the United States. Before leaving for Rochester he cabled her.

> WILL YOU MARRY ME
> AND GO TO SOUTH AMERICA?

Her response was:

> MEET COUSIN ELEANOR IN TOKYO

Dad found this reply confusing and annoying. What kind of response was that to a marriage proposal?

He headed by ship back to America. When the ship stopped in Hong Kong, he learned the Japanese had invaded Manchuria. By the time the ship reached Shanghai pandemonium had seized its stock market. Manchuria was the economic heartland of China with its coal and iron. Clearly China could not defend herself and would be open to further Japanese conquest. It was considered unlikely any European nation would be willing to go to war with Japan to save China.

When Dad arrived in Tokyo he met Cousin Eleanor, known as Audie, Mom's first cousin.

"Are you going to marry Milly?" Audie asked.

"That's my question to you" he countered.

Neither knew Mom's decision. However, Mom had given up her job escorting the Japanese boy to Japan and passed it on to Audie. If Mom had decided not to go back to China, perhaps she was going to marry him. Dad cabled Mom with his plans for arrival in Rochester and continued on his voyage.

Audie joined him on the steamer back to the States, having completed her job escorting the Japanese child. On board ship they met a young man, George McHutchin, who was good company. Audie fell in love with George but his company would not allow him to marry until after he had worked abroad five years. They had to separate while he returned to England and resigned his job. As Mom had noticed, single unattached women were snatched up quickly in the Orient. George and Audie later married and moved to Kenya where they had two children, one of whom, Marny, reappeared in our lives much later.

In New York City Mom struggled with a dilemma. She had not seen Dad in over a year and she knew she did not feel towards him the way she had felt with her high school sweetheart Wink. She also now realized she did not want a barren life of just work, even in an exciting environment. She wanted companionship and children and surmised, at twenty-six, there might not be too many more offers. Her home life had been so bad marriage seemed somewhat threatening. Dad was something of an enigma as she had spent so little time with him. Mom wrote to her friend Eleanor Breed about her reservations. Did they love each other enough for the marriage to last? The wrong marriage would be worse than no marriage. She decided to go to Batavia, the last stop of Dad's train before its arrival in Rochester, board the train and talk to him.

She found him in the dining car having breakfast. Fighting his astonishment at seeing her there, he casually pulled up a chair.

"Milly, have you had breakfast yet?"

We don't know what transpired between them but, when the train arrived in Rochester, they were engaged. Milly later wrote she made a pact with herself before the marriage: she would do anything to have a happy marriage and she would always say "yes" to any plans Dad made. She would be a trooper. It took years, and many trying experiences, before we all learned how difficult it was to be a trooper.

These two world travelers said their marriage vows on December 14th, 1931, and headed to Santiago, Chile. Dad was twenty-seven and Mom twenty-six. It was a marriage based on companionship, adventure and a future family. They hoped love would come later.

Quickly they came upon a serious problem—they could not have intercourse and did not understand why. After struggling to find a solution on their own, they consulted a doctor as soon as they arrived in Chile. Mom underwent a small operation to correct a vaginal blockage, and it solved the problem. From then on, whenever our family experienced difficulties, Mom would say: "Take it to the doctor"—a reference which meant to an expert.

Their apartment in Santiago looked out directly on the Plaza des Armas, a park in the middle of the city. Parents pushed strollers at almost all hours and relaxed at cozy little cafes. The very first day, when she took the elevator down in order to go exploring, she met Ann Hathaway who later became a good friend. Mom was extremely out-going and made friends more easily than Dad, who was naturally a little shy.

Ann Hathaway was Anglo-Chilean and claimed Chileans were the best-dressed women in the world. She taught Mom how to shop for outfits, not just individual pieces of clothing, and how to work with a seamstress. They shopped and shopped and shopped but bought nothing until they found a completely coordinated outfit—dress, shoes, stockings, hat and gloves. Ann emphasized the difference between fashion and style. Fashion was the current fad, but style was individual. With Ann's help, Mom developed her own sense of style and never lost it. Ann said one needed time but not a lot of money to dress well. Ann said working girls dressed in black because they didn't have the time necessary to shop successfully. Dad had reason to be proud of Mom's looks, and he was. She believed strongly every woman could look well if she put the effort into it—and she did! For the rest of her life, clothes were important to her, and she remained stylish whenever she left the house.

A business friend of my father's, Gene Falkenburg, came from a tennis family and encouraged them to play tennis together at the Stade Francais in the Santiago suburbs. Mom learned to play well and incidentally lost some weight. The Falkenburg's son Bob later won the Wimbledon men's singles title in 1948 and their daughter Jinx won tennis titles and became a famous model and TV host in the 1940s. Mom received excellent instruction from them. She remained active athletically the rest of her life playing tennis, swimming, horseback riding and doing whatever else Dad enjoyed. These activities were part of the pact she made with herself before marrying—she would do everything he wanted to do. She soon began to enjoy these activities herself.

Mom struggled with cooking. She had no recipe book, and she hadn't learned enough Spanish to describe what she was attempting to do to her maid. So a friend sent her a woman familiar with American cooking and just told the cook to do whatever she thought Mom would like without specific instructions. Dad said it worked well although sometimes he would come home and find Mom cackling like a chicken or flapping her wings to get an idea across. Mom never became a good cook, but I don't think she really cared. She liked having someone cook for her and preferred devoting her time to the table settings and guests.

While in Chile, Mom received a letter from her brother Ray. He was considering getting a divorce from his wife Elsie. He decided to wait because of fierce opposition from his parents, but he divorced shortly after his parents died. "Divorce is all right if you have no children," Mom told Dad. "I think our marriage will last so it is time to start our family." She now looked forward to staying home and taking care of future children. Maybe her days of adventure had ended.

Dad followed geopolitical news carefully and the Great Depression hit hard at Chile's principal exports, nitrates and copper. Unemployment raged and inflation wrecked the currency. From the time they arrived in January until they left in October the exchange rate rose from eight pesos to one US dollar to sixty-four pesos to one US dollar. People who were paid locally became poverty-stricken. Pawn shops did a booming business. Mom bought a diamond watch there for just a few US dollars—what was one person's loss was someone else's gain. The middle class became smaller as inflation robbed them of much of the value of their incomes and many were pushed into poverty. The value of the peso dropped so much the Falkenbergs, who were paid in pesos, left for California. Circumstances were ripe for revolution.

There were two fairly bloodless revolts in six months and then a third. One night the telephone rang while they were asleep. Dad's boss's wife, Minina, was calling. The following is what he wrote in *Milly*:

37

*"Get up! Get up!" Minina said hysterically on the telephone... "The Communists are coming! They have overpowered the police, and the mob has set fire to the Cathedral. They are plundering the stores! Now they are coming this way burning and looting! Nothing can stop them..."*

*I handed Milly the phone.*

*"The silver?" I heard Milly ask. "Bury the silver? O.K. We'll be ready and wait for your call. Yes, sandwiches." She hung up and sat on the bed stunned.*

*After a moment she repeated numbly the words storming through her head. "Get up! Dress warmly. Bury your silver. Make sandwiches. Wait for us to call again."*

For an hour Mom and Dad stayed up drinking coffee, but there were no disturbances. They wondered if the call had been a joke and eventually went back to bed. In the morning all remained calm, and the morning paper was on the stoop. The entire newspaper, except for the ads, was a reprint of Alice in Wonderland. It was the editor's way of saying the paper had been censored. Monday morning a red flag with a hammer and sickle flew over the Presidential Palace. Business was at a standstill. Two weeks later the military regained control but this time it was not without bloodshed. It was rumored they executed three hundred students.

Dad's replacement in the Philippines suddenly become ill and, in the fall, Dad received instructions to return to the Philippines. Mom was not happy with this change because she was five months pregnant and she knew she would be seasick on the voyage there. She needed to be a trooper. On the ship she took to her bunk and mostly emerged only when they were in port. The voyage took two months to go up the South American coast (twelve days just to Panama), to San

Francisco (one-week layover to put on a new crew), Hawaii, Japan, Shanghai, Hong Kong and finally Manila. They were embarking on a new phase in their lives, having a family, but would it suit them as much as the first adventures?

As soon as they arrived in Manila, Mom set to work getting a doctor and hospital in case she should need them earlier than expected. Soon she had located a rental house, furnishings and a Filipino cook. Over the years she became extremely efficient at finding the necessities in each new location. Dad always dressed properly which in the tropical Philippines meant a fresh white suit and white shoes every day. His clothes necessitated daily washing but Mom did not want to do this job herself. It became obvious they needed a lavandera. She found one on the cook's recommendation. They barely noticed a five-year-old girl who ran behind the lavandera's skirts each time she saw Mom or Dad. He told what happened next this way:

> *One day he (the cook) asked if he could borrow five pesos (US $2.50) as an advance on his salary. He said he wanted it to get married, and that was the cost of the license and the priest's fees. This sounded reasonable, and we gave him the money. Next day he asked for the next day off for his wedding and, please, for the day off for the lavandera also. Again, we agreed. Our surprise came on the wedding day. Not only was the cook lavishly dressed but so was the lavandera—in bridal gown! The little girl served as flower girl.*
>
> *Later we learned that our cook had been born in the country and had never before had five pesos in cash. Therefore he could not marry, and the little girl was their much-loved child.*

My older brother, Robert Gordon Junior, was born in Manila on March 22, 1933, in St. Luke's Hospital. Custom dictated that mother and son remain in the hospital for a week and then return home with a hospital nurse. The nurse would stay with them for another week and teach the mother and the recently hired amah (nanny) how to care for the baby. Of course, the cook recommended the new amah, Felisa, and she turned out to be the sister of the lavandera. Felisa stayed with us for years and was practically a mother to young Bob.

With three servants Mom was able to resume a more active social life. She determined to spend one hour each day playing with Bob which gave her plenty of free time. She volunteered at St. Luke's Hospital and even worked in real estate for a short time. Her skill at finding necessities for her own family translated into help for other new arrivals. On weekends she would sit at the Polo Club with other young mothers sipping lemonade and watching the men play softball while Felisa watched Bob in the playground. After the softball game Dad would walk over to the playground, pick up Bob, and take him swimming. Bob learned to swim about the same time he learned to walk. Often, after a family siesta, Dad and Mom would go back to the club to watch a polo game and enjoy the tea-dance. They would return home in the evening for dinner, as the club evening meal was too expensive for them.

Young Bob suffered from many of the illnesses of the tropics and childhood. He developed prickly heat from continuous perspiration in the moist, hot weather, impetigo (a fungus growing under the skin), then conjunctivitis (an eye infection) before coming down with whooping cough. Felisa slept on the floor of his room so she could pick him up whenever he had a coughing spell.

My younger brother Bruce Gordon was born on September 4, 1934. He stayed in the hospital for four weeks to shield him from Bob's whooping cough. Bruce was a welcome addition to the family but there were increasing financial pressures. Dad's salary had suffered two ten percent cuts because of the Great Depression, and now there were four family members to support. To save money, they fired the cook and gave up their membership in the Polo Club. But firing the cook, whose salary was low, saved little money and giving up their membership in the Polo Club drastically effected their life style. They soon changed their minds and reversed both actions—they would manage somehow.

One afternoon when our parents were away Felisa was playing with Bob in our backyard. Baby Bruce was supposedly asleep in a back room but Felisa heard his cry coming from the front of the house. She ran towards the sound, but his cry now came from the street. She spied a teenage boy hurrying away with the baby held loosely in his arms. Fearing he might drop the boy, Felisa ran up behind him and grabbed the baby. The boy ran off. When our parents came home, they called the police who found the kidnapper, a handicapped Filipino-American who had previously snatched babies. Filipinos call kidnapping "the American crime" because the son of the famous pilot, Charles Lindbergh, was kidnapped for ransom in America just two years earlier.

The family lived in a Filipino nipa style house on low stilts with a bathroom but without a tub or hot water. The house had no windows but kapiz shutters. We couldn't afford such food as cornflakes or beef but there were local fruits, vegetables, chicken, fish and eggs. Kodak paid for our medical care which was important because of the prevalence of dengue fever, malaria, amoebic dysentery, leprosy, cholera, impetigo and fungi. We slept under mosquito netting which kept the mosquitoes out but the heat in. The netting had to stay away from your body so mosquitoes couldn't bite you through it. We avoided undulant fever by drinking canned condensed milk (I pasteurized our raw milk on our farm in

41

New Jersey when I had children because I feared undulant fever). Mom looked forward to a time when we might move to a better climate.

Bruce clearly remembers the arrival of the first commercial airplane to cross the Pacific, a Pan Am Clipper, when it landed in Manila bay. A large crowd turned out for the event. Bruce and Bob boarded the plane and climbed into its nose where they had their picture taken. To cross the Pacific the flying boat had to refuel so it stopped at Wake Island. The island had been uninhabited until the US Marines built cement catch-basins to capture fresh rainwater and provide a water supply. Then it became a vital refueling stop without which the Pam Am Clipper would not have been able to make its flight. Wake was of such strategic importance that the Japanese attacked and captured it at the very beginning of WWII.

In 1936 Dad had been overseas for five years and was scheduled for home leave. Since Manila is about half way around the world from Rochester, the family booked round-the-world tickets starting with the German ship M.V. Scharnhorst through the Suez to New York. Most of the ship's passengers were German or Japanese and Mom and Dad saw a different world view than the one they were familiar with in the American Philippines. Any mention of Hitler, Mussolini or the Emperor was with pride and belligerence. Our parents' concern about possible war increased. Dad wrote a small book, *Sonny Sees the World**, about this trip. Sonny was Bob's childhood name, and the book was about his adventures in the round-the-world trip.

When they arrived at the home office in Rochester, Dad asked for a transfer out of the Orient. He felt his family was unsafe in the current political situation and it was time for a change—a new location in a climate healthier for his

---

* Gordon, Robert M. *Sonny Sees the World. A Story Told By His Daddy.* 1937

children. Mom's parents were thrilled to see their only grand-children, but the family stayed with her parents for only two days before moving in with her brother Ralph and his wife.

Dad's best friend and a fellow football player at the University of Rochester had been Max Dunn. He lived in Mendon outside of Rochester. While they were driving around the area, Max pointed out a small farm he thought might interest Dad. It could be a port in the storm in the future if he ever returned to Rochester. Dad expressed interest and asked Max to let him know if it came on the market.

They spent three weeks in Rochester, taking time to see many of their friends, and then headed back to the Philippines via Vancouver. The Japanese had occupied Manchuria in 1931 and were now threatening the rest of China. In Shanghai their friends anxiously watched the Japanese advance.

On board ship between Shanghai and Hong Kong the boys went up to the ship's nursery to play and found it occupied by soldiers. When Mom went to investigate, an Indian Sikh in uniform barred the door. In a previous trip, she learned, Chinese pirates had seized the ship. An advanced group had traveled in steerage with the balance boarding from their junks (Chinese ships). They had looted the ship and robbed the passengers, then escaped in the junks back to the main-land. On this trip, the Captain locked the steerage passengers behind iron gates and posted armed guards in the bridge and engine rooms. It seems the nursery was the only place to house the guards.

After the family docked in Hong Kong, Dad and Mom learned that T. V. Soong, then Finance Minister of China under President Chiang Kai-shek, had been among the passengers. He was traveling under the name of Mr. Chang, and he had twelve secretaries with him of the same name. They occupied separate staterooms and each night Mr. Soong would sleep in a different cabin. The Shanghai newspapers reported the

Finance Minister was flying to Hong Kong and thus established his cover. T. V. Soong was the brother of the famous Soong sisters and brother-in-law of Sun Yat-sen and Chiang Kai-shek.

It delighted Bob to be back in the Philippines. For him it was home. Felisa was waiting for him. As he was now four, Mom enrolled him in the American School where he could regularly interact with other children and learn some discipline.

Dad was an excellent bedtime story teller. His specialty was a series of Red Feather stories about a white boy who was captured and adopted by American Indians. Red Feather went on many hunting parties and war parties with the Indians and Dad had an endless array of stories about his many adventures. Mother gave a birthday party based on the Red Feather stories where the young guests came as cowboys and Bruce and Bob as Indians, wearing loin cloths with feather headdresses. Dad provided them with toy bows and arrows and they shot at the target of a bear on a Canadian railway poster tacked on a tree. Whether or not they hit the target, they got a hot dog of bear meat for lunch. The boys loved any adventure story.

One afternoon Dad planned to take the boys sailing in Manila Bay. He made them some fishing poles, and they were excited about fishing off the boat. When the time came to leave, Bruce changed his mind and said he didn't want to go fishing. Dad brought his pole anyway. On board, Bruce would not leave Dad's side. Bob put bread on his pole and fished while Bruce watched. Dad concluded Bruce was physically conservative and would avoid fights. Time would prove him wrong. Bruce was simply cautious whereas Bob tended to jump in on impulse. Bruce later became an excellent fisherman and pilot.

Mom was always ready to join Dad on any trip but their experience at the cave at Wau-Wau Beach amazes me. A group of American friends hired a bus and rode to the little village of Nasugbu on the South China Sea. They rented outrigger canoes and villagers to row them out to the beach and cave. Their guide dared the good swimmers to follow him into the cave where they swam in total darkness except for the phosphorescent green glow of their kicks. Dad wrote a poem about their experience, a portion of which follows:

*...Around this turn*
*Just when the ceiling dips*

*The greenish daylight shows below your feet.*
*A hole leads to the sea.*
*The tide and mermaids here go in andout,*
*And so, my friends, can we!*

*The hole is small but big enough for one;*
*The passage three feet thick.*
*Breath deep, dive down, swim hard and come up slow.*
*The walls forbid you kick.*

*Outside the surf is rough and hides the hole.*
*Keep way! To reach our cove*
*Swim 'round the point. There is no fear of sharks*
*Good luck! And down he dove!*

*A youth who fears adventure fears to live*
*And from the world retreats.*
*Although our friends turned back, With you I go!*
*My wife now thrice repeats.*

*To me the wiggling green sunlight below*
*Enticed like moths the flame.*
*Deep breaths I took, then toward that fairy light*
*I dove for game or shame.*

*How fine the hole! So deep! Beware the walls!*
*My muscles soon got tight*
*My eyes and lungs seemed crushed when like a bomb*
*Burst forth a world of light!*

*Up, up and out I swam for air and life.*
*How glorious the game!*
*I was alone at sea. The breaking waves*
*The rocks hid whence I came.*

*My lonely fear for her a moment's wait*
*Make long my other life.*
*Like Venus from the sea splashing, gasping*
*For air, up popped my wife!*

*No rest! A half-hour's swim around the point,*
*The jagged rocks to flee.*
*No flippered feet, lifesaving belt or boat.*
*What lucky fools were we!*

In August 1937 the Japanese invasion of China reached the International Settlement in Shanghai. Foreigners were ordered out and many refugees, including some of Mom and Dad's friends, arrived in Manila. Our family had taken short trips up to Camp Labi, an abandoned Army camp in the hills run by the YMCA which had cabins you could rent. Dad developed a family evacuation plan to the camp in case the Japanese invaded the Philippines. He put a month's supply of canned milk and other foods and necessities in the back of our car and kept it there.

When they received word from their friend Max Dunn back in Rochester that the small farm in Mendon had become available they decided they needed a safe home base in the United States. They had to mortgage their life insurance to buy the farm, but they did. They even arranged, through

Max, to have small evergreen seedlings planted by the Boy Scouts for the future.

Mom was happy with their family and felt it was time to have a luxury baby—they felt they couldn't afford another one, but time was flying. On January 7th, 1938, I, Ann Elizabeth Gordon, joined the family. I had almost no hair as a baby and when it came in, it was a very light blond. Bruce and I were what was then referred to as tow heads.

Mom wanted to be sure people knew I was a girl, so she taped a bow to my head. We have a picture of me on a sofa entitled *Snow White and the Seven Dwarfs* showing how creative Mom was. I sat on a white sheet with seven dwarf dolls around me. Bob and Bruce were somewhat displaced by the new baby, both literally and figuratively. They took a room downstairs on the servants' floor and I moved into the nursery upstairs.

When summer came Mom took her little family and servants to Baguio in the mountains where it was cooler. Now the boys were old enough to play outside. When she wanted them to come back in she would go out on the porch and call "wah-wah-wah-wah-WHA-wah," an old American Indian call our family often used. After a while, when she stepped out on the porch the natives would join her in the call. Later in Manila she met an American anthropologist who described how the Igorots called to each other much as did the American Indians long ago. It sounded like *wah-wah-wah-wah-Wah-wah* and Mom thought it was the call the Igorots had learned from her.

When it came time for Felisa's vacation, she asked if Bob, then five, could come with her. With our parents' approval they went by bus to her village. He loved the trip, and learned how the villagers grew their own food. He rode a carabao (water buffalo), and slept on the upper floor of the stilt house over the chickens and pigs. Felisa showed him how to clean his teeth with sand from just off the beach where the waves break and the sand is extremely fine. He felt he belonged because she belonged and there was sadness on both their parts when they had to return to Manila.

Bob established a strong tie to the Philippines which he has maintained into his eighties. Most Filipinos are Catholic and Felisa imparted some of her faith to him. She was not, however, permitted to teach him to make the sign of the cross. Mother was somewhat anti-Catholic but not as much as her father had been. I always felt Felisa's gift of faith to Bob was a blessing. I was too young at the time for her to influence me and have had to find my own way.

One night when Dad was telling a Red Feather story downstairs in the boys' room, he heard Mom scream. She had gone into the upstairs bathroom without turning on the light and suddenly noticed there was someone else in the room. When she screamed, a man fled down the stairs and bumped into Dad heading up. The man escaped into the tall grass field outside with Dad right behind him. In the dark, Dad lost sight of him, then suddenly he tripped over the man hiding in grass. The chase resumed and Dad, being an ex-football player, tackled him and brought him back to the house. The thief was a former cook he had fired. The boys were excited and asked if he would be shot at sunrise—of course not, but he was arrested.

Although they didn't know it at the time, this was probably the happiest time of Mom and Dad's lives. They had a lovely little family and time for many interesting pleasures because they had inexpensive and helpful servants. They later referred to this period as Camelot. But the world was catching up with them. Dad felt unsafe in Manila and Mom wanted a better climate for her children.

# IV

In March 1939 Dad received his requested transfer to Honolulu, Hawaii. He was enthusiastic because he considered it a dream assignment as the warehouse manager of Kodak Hawaii. Mom wanted to move to a gentler climate where she thought her family would be healthier, but she realized she would miss the servants. Then she got a call from the Red Cross asking if we would bring a fifteen-year-old girl with us as an amah during the voyage. Lynn was a Japanese-Filipina going to join her Japanese mother in Hawaii. Mom delightfully accepted as she knew Lynn could help on the voyage.

Leaving Manila was rough on Bob Jr. He was six, had started school, and had many friends. He also was deeply attached to Felisa—she had been almost a mother to him. He could not understand why she didn't come with us to Honolulu. Probably she simply wanted to stay in the Philippines with her own family, but I am sure Bob thought of her as part of our family. For him, Manila was home. Bob has often been disappointed and felt unfairly treated by life while I have felt unusually fortunate. Our different inclinations may have begun here with Bob sensing he had lost something which I never had and thus couldn't lose. Since I was only a one-year-old, I did not remember the Philippines as home. We never saw Felisa again.

Bruce grew up in Bob's shadow. Bob did everything first, was more responsible and more mature. Of course, Bob was a year and a half older than Bruce, but Bruce did not always look at it that way. He knew he could not do all the things Bob did. Mom and Dad talked about Bruce someday becoming a farmer and Bob a diplomat. Bruce became Bob's tag-a-long and was nicknamed *Me-Too* because he said these words so often.

The voyage to Honolulu took us to Hong Kong, Shanghai (yes, America was not yet at war with Japan, although China was), Kobe and Yokohama before heading south across the Pacific. The weather in the northern Pacific was cold and the sea turbulent. Not only was Mom seasick but this time the boys and Lynn were too. It was a great relief when we pulled up to the pier at Aloha Tower. The smell of plumeria blossoms wafted through gentle breezes. Bougainvilleas of mesmerizing pastel colors cascaded over walls. Hawaiian music massaged our senses as we watched the hula dancers who greeted the ship. And Kodak friends welcomed us and helped us get settled. We had, indeed, come to paradise.

Mom was her usual efficient self, rapidly finding us a cottage to rent in the Manoa Valley and within three months locating a house to buy in Wailupe between Diamond Head and Koko Head. Lynn spent a little time with her mother but then came back to us as she preferred our home. Mom said Lynn was almost more trouble than she was worth, but she kept her because Mom had never taken care of three children by herself and needed the help.

Bruce loved Hawaii. There was so much to explore. To reach the beach was only a short stroll down a lane and there was no end of things to do. The weather was beautiful most of the time and even when it rained we would often have liquid sunshine—the sun shone at the same time it was raining. He could go crabbing, fishing, swimming, and climb trees. One day he climbed up on the roof of our house to figure out how our solar water heater worked—yes, we used the sun to heat our water in 1940! He stood up just as a fighter plane flew by so low he could see the pilot. The plane pulled up to fly over the trees and Bruce dreamed of flying himself.

When I was two, I was the beneficiary of one of Mom's best birthday parties which we have on film. She had taken an angel food cake pan, covered it with paper, and then frosted the paper to look like a cake. Inside the cake she put LIVE BIRDS. When I cut the cake, with her help, the birds flew out! Another time she made a similar cake but put baby chicks inside—then the guests could each take a baby chick home with them. We kept some chicks and a duck, Donald Quack Quack. *He* turned out to be a *she* and laid eggs. Honolulu was a place of great freedom for children due to the wonderful weather. We could wander around with very few clothes, get dirty and then just shower outside to clean off. Of course, we seldom wore shoes.

Honolulu did not turn out to be the paradise for her Mom had expected. Yes, the weather was glorious, but she was used to lots of servants and now she had only one young girl to help with a family of three young children. Lynn eventually had a baby, married and left. Now Mom had all the work to do and she had little time for herself. Mom began having serious headaches she attributed to exhaustion and an allergy to the kiawe trees growing nearby. In the years to come, headaches would be a recurring problem. Could they have been migraines? We never knew. Perhaps she was suffering from depression. She would have happily gone back to the Philippines except the rest of the family loved Honolulu and Dad's job was there. In his journals Dad wrote about their discussions concerning the headaches but she didn't complain to others outside the family. It was important to be a trooper and always have a smile on your face.

One day I fell face down near the ocean's edge, and a receding wave took me with it. Lynn quickly grabbed me, but it terrified Mom. I never developed the love of swimming the rest of the family enjoyed and have wondered whether my aversion to swimming was due to this incident or my dislike of the feel of cold water. Of course, we all became good swimmers, but I never loved the water the way my brothers did.

Dad described a more serious incident in his book *Milly*:

> *A few months later Bruce was invited to go fishing one Sunday morning with the little boy next door and his father, who had a rowboat down at the beach. The others of us went to church, but when we came home, our neighbor's wife was hysterical. The rowboat had been washed up on the beach empty! Quickly Milly ran one way up the beach and I the other. The seawall around a fishpond allowed me to walk out a little way toward the reef, and there indeed I saw a man's body in the water, face down. I called out, and someone came running. We dragged him out, and I tried artificial respiration, but it was too late. Our neighbor was dead-someone called the Fire Department.*

The boys were still missing so Dad sent Bob up the beach calling out for Bruce. A man came out of his beach house and told Bob his brother was not in that direction, and he should go back. Bob met Bruce just as he reached the crowd. Bob hugged him heartily. Bruce at first did not understand the uproar because he did not know about the accident. He later explained that a friend of Mr. Linjap's had shown up and wanted to go fishing with him. Mr. Linjap told the boys to play on the beach by themselves until it was their turn. The men rowed out and evidently one of them dove into the water and hit his head on the coral—the other jumped in to rescue him but was not a good enough swimmer. Bruce sympathized with the Linjap boy who had lost his father. Might we also lose our father? Our family was shaken because for a half-hour we had thought Bruce might be dead. He was only six years old, and he had already been kidnapped and possibly drowned.

We all remember wonderful short family trips in Honolulu—to Hanauma Bay, to the top of Koko Head, to the Blow Hole, to the Pali, and to the Mormon Temple. We would take snacks and make it a day, usually including swimming and hiking. Bruce developed a reputation for being a klutz and perpetually messy. One day when Mom asked him to clean out his pockets, she found fourteen items including a knife, button, stone, pencil and flashlight bulb. He also became rather sneaky. Since he was not as strong as his older brother, he had to use his brain sometimes to get what he wanted. Dad told the following story:

> *One morning Bruce asked if I [Dad] would take him to Fritzie's house, he had left his cap pistol there. I could not do it that day, but perhaps his mother could. He had already tried her, and he disappeared. A little later he noticed that Sonny [Bob] had a pistol just like his [because we always bought them two of everything]. There was a silence before Bruce grabbed the gun, and a fight started, both boys claiming ownership. By sheer strength Sonny kept it. After a pause Bruce demanded, "Has it got a star on it?" Sonny turned it over and over, but there was no star. "Then it's mine!" Bruce shouted and grabbed the gun. Sonny let him have it. Milly saw through the trick before I did; neither gun ever had a star.*

In the summer of 1941 Dad's concern about war with Japan became so acute he booked Mom and the three kids on a trip to the mainland for safety. Japan had expelled most foreigners, and she was buying large quantities of scrap metal from America. The more secretive Japan became the more convinced Dad was she was about to strike. In May we had a gala send-off at the dock with many friends coming down to the pier and piling us high with leis. Passengers threw streamers from the ship's railing, a band played and someone sang "Aloha Oe." The boys especially enjoyed watching the young beachboys dive for coins. In those days the Matson Line of passenger ships regularly made gala send offs and arrivals for their vessels for promotional reasons. Kodak also sponsored hula shows near Waikiki Beach for publicity.

From Los Angeles, Mom took us to the Holt Ranch in San Luis Obispo, California, a working ranch with paying guests. The boys helped with the horses, cows, dogs, ducks, cats, pigs and chickens on the ranch. They learned to ride, shoot and do farm chores. Bob thoroughly enjoyed learning new skills and developed a sense of confidence. I also learned to ride although I couldn't mount my pony by myself.

Mom's health improved, which seemed to confirm the thesis her headaches in Wailupe were due to the kiawe trees, but she also had few responsibilities cooking, cleaning and caring for the children. The staff took care of most of these activities. To Mom's delight, in July Dad joined us at the ranch. Most of the single women at the ranch were divorced, and they found it hard to believe Mom was there fleeing the threat of war, not a failed marriage. Dad participated in the barbecues, riding and square dances for a short time before taking us with him to Rochester. He needed to report to the Kodak home office again.

In Rochester we visited many relatives, including Grandpa Gordon. Our other three grandparents had died during the preceding year. Grandpa Gordon was the only grandparent I ever met, and he lived until I was a senior in high school. Max Dunn took us for a drive to Mendon to see the farm our parents had purchased while in Manila. The seedling trees the Boy Scouts had planted were still only eight inches tall.

Dad took a short trip to Washington, D.C. where he was interviewed for a position in Naval intelligence. Bob took a train trip by himself (he was eight years old) up to New Hampshire to visit his Manila friend Sally Day. Mom left for New York to see her friend Esther Wood Brady with whom she had made her initial trip to Europe many years earlier. Then we all reunited in Rochester, bought a convertible and drove back to California where we put the car on a ship and sailed back to Hawaii. The Japanese were sending a peace mission to Washington, so it appeared to be safe enough to return to Honolulu.

As soon as we returned, the boys re-enrolled in the University of Hawaii Teachers' College Experimental School. Lynn came to help Mom for two weeks and then returned to her family. Mom's headaches came back, as did the increased responsibilities. One day Mom received a call from Bob's school—he was not in class. It turned out when he was dropped off at the curb, he did not go in. He had a can of vegetables to donate to the needy and he did not want to be seen carrying the can—it was unmanly. He was found still sitting on the curb.

Not long after our return Dad received a letter offering him a commission in the Naval reserves. His interview in Washington had gone well, and the offer was what he wanted-ed. However, the Kodak office manager, Fritz Herman, asked him to decline the commission because Fritz was already a Naval reservist and, if there were war, Fritz would be called up at once. Dad would have to head the office. He refused the commission.

The morning of December 7th, 1941, a Sunday, was the kind on Hawaiian postcards; sunny with soft breezes wafting ocean smells in from the beach. Bob and Bruce had ventured out to hunt crabs with their BB guns. Dad was mowing the lawn and Mom was cleaning up from breakfast and listening to the radio. An announcer broke in "The Japanese are attacking Pearl Harbor. This is not a drill. This is the real McCoy!" Mom could hardly believe it, but the announcer repeated it. She called to Dad to come in, then ran out to fetch the boys. We all gathered around the radio.

The announcer declared martial law was in effect. All essential personnel were to report to work immediately, and all reservists were now on active duty. Dad drove to his office on the other side of Diamond Head, closer to Pearl Harbor. He arrived there just as a Navy jeep pulled up, followed by an Army truck. Both services were there to requisition Kodak movie and x-ray film. After allocating supplies, he went up on the roof to see what was happening. Black smoke rose above Pearl Harbor. He spied planes circling and diving amid more billows of smoke as the second attack wave came in. Suddenly he heard an explosion behind him. Turning, he saw five more explosions in quick succession. There was no airplane overhead. Then he realized the explosions came from American anti-aircraft shells fired at the Japanese planes but missing and exploding when they hit the ground. It was time to get off the roof. Later he learned a battery had failed to set the fuses on their shells to explode in mid-air. Unfortunately, there were casualties on the ground from friendly fire, one of whom was the Japanese-American lady from whom he regularly bought cigarettes.

Back in Wailupe, Army trucks had pulled up and soldiers had begun installing coils of barbed wire, building pill boxes with sand bags and setting up machine guns in the area between our house and the beach. Wailupe would be a natural landing place for Japanese troops if they invaded the island. About a quarter of a mile out is a reef, and beyond it water deep enough for large ships. Troops could come by ship up to the reef and then wade in. Behind our house ran Kalanianaole Highway, the main route giving access to the opposite side of the island of Oahu. The only other route was over the Pali, much too narrow and steep for military vehicles. On the other side of the highway from our house was a wide, sparsely inhabited valley which would make an ideal landing place for parachutists. The military feared the Japanese would coordinate a landing on the beach with a parachute landing in the valley, thus cutting the island in half.

A Grant tank arrived at the beach and fascinated the boys. When Mom called them in to lunch, they were reluctant to leave the excitement outside. While we were eating, there was a burst of machine gun fire when the soldiers tested their guns. Mom nearly dropped the bowl of peas she was carrying. In an attempt to calm herself down, she decided to paint the front door. As she was finishing, she glanced to her left and saw an American soldier with a bayonet stalking across our garden. She almost fell off the ladder. So much for calming down! She panicked easily and this time the circumstances warranted it.

When Dad returned from his office, he decided to investigate the defenses near our house. Turning to Bob he said: "You need to be a man now, come with me." Together they went down to the beach to see the military preparations. Circumstances were placing more pressure on Bob than most young children carry. Eventually I came to understand Mom and Dad expected a lot of Bob at an early age because he was the oldest child and a boy.

Our neighbor, Dr. Ogawa, was Japanese-American and his wife a Canadian nurse. He was almost sick with grief. His native country had attacked his adopted country. Their son Gilbert was Bob's friend and their daughter Janie was my friend. Prominent Japanese (such as Dr. Ogawa), those born in Japan (Issei), those who had recently traveled to Japan, and those who worked for Japanese companies were under suspicion. As he had feared, the military police soon arrested Dr. Ogawa. Our father testified to his loyalty and Dr. Ogawa was released. Many Japanese-Americans on the Islands had similar experiences. Although it was a difficult time for them, internment was not widespread. Mainland Japanese-Americans on the west coast suffered mass relocation in camps for most of the war. Authorities told them it was to protect them from the rest of the population who hated and feared Japanese. In Hawaii over a third of the population was of Japanese ancestry. Interning them all would be impossible and they were a valuable part of the community.

A curfew and complete blackout started the very first night. We had only a few blankets because Hawaiian weather was usually warm, and one seldom needed them. Mom and Dad put the blankets we had over the windows in the kitchen downstairs and turned off the lights in all the other rooms. Dad went up to a local horse stable where we used to ride to secure feed bags, but all the empty bags had already been taken so we used pillowcases to make our sandbags. He constructed a make-shift bomb shelter using our tubs and sandbags. If there were an air raid, we were to lie on the floor under the sinks with sandbags around us. As our house was close to the beach, we had no basement. Our telephone line was spliced to provide telephone access for the soldiers. Residents were told not to make telephone calls anyway so the lines could be open for military calls.

There was not much to do after dark so Dad took us into the darkened living room and told us a Red Feather story. Mom put us to bed early. Then they went outside to breathe the night air and talk. They were avid smokers, but martial law banned smoking outdoors at night due to the light of the cigarettes. They had to discuss their options. Should the whole family stay together in Hawaii and risk invasion and possible imprisonment or should they take the chance of having Mom and the three children join a naval convoy through enemy waters in an attempt to reach the mainland?

I was upstairs in my bedroom but not sleepy because it was still early. I turned on my light to play. A brilliant shaft of light cut through my window and beyond to where Dad and Mom were sitting. Dad rushed up the stairs. I thought he was furious although now I think he was primarily scared for our safety. Nervous soldiers surrounded our house, prepared to shoot at almost anything . Dad promptly removed all the light bulbs upstairs. I cried because I knew I had done something terribly wrong, but I didn't understand what it was.

An imminent Japanese invasion was on everyone's mind. The military Governor's will was law. New US currency was printed with HAWAII stamped on it and our old dollars turned in for the new ones. If the Japanese conquered the islands, they would be prevented from using US dollars to buy supplies elsewhere in the world. The banks collected $200 million of the old currency and burned it. After the war, the overprinted currency was requisitioned by the government and also destroyed, although some people saved a little as souvenirs. I still have a HAWAII dollar bill and so do my brothers.

Monday morning all schools were closed. Mom made some gingerbread with whipped cream and gave it to the soldiers on the beach who were primarily Japanese-American reservists. The boys loved watching all their preparations. The Grant tank caused quite a sensation wherever it went. Rumors abounded—Japanese saboteurs had poisoned the water supply; parachutists had landed in the sugarcane fields; submarines had put spies ashore. We were to please report anyone flashing lights out to ships at sea. The boys found all the activity quite exciting.

Grocery stores were mobbed when they were opened. By military law, food purchases were limited, such as two bars of soap to one person, or six oranges per person. Food was sold regardless of national origin—Japanese shoppers were not discriminated against. Within two weeks most food restrictions were lifted, but many things were simply not available. Prices rose considerably. At first, gasoline was not sold, then it was rationed to ten gallons per month. Dad needed to drive to his office daily and this law made life difficult. Car pools became a necessity. Schools did not open for weeks. Liquor stores and bars were closed.

Mom was not the only one who was extremely nervous. She wrote:

> *The slightest irregularity in one's conduct was cause for arrest and even shooting. One rumour told of a man near a fort walking along in view of a guard when the wind blew his hat off. He leaned over behind a hedge to get it and was shot. The machine gunners on our compound kidded each other about their nervousness. Several times in the night they had shot at creaking palm trees making odd-shaped shadows in the night. All during the week the wind was unusually blustery, and excitement was at a feverish pitch.*

Christmas was approaching, and our parents attempted to make life as normal as possible. Christmas trees were usually shipped from the mainland so there was considerable question whether they would make it to Hawaii. On Christmas morning there one was waiting to greet us with decorations and all. We eagerly tore open our presents, then put on our holiday clothes and drove off to wish our friends a Merry Christmas—a family tradition. After a few visits with somewhat forced merriment we stopped for lunch at a restaurant. Dad told us this was so Mom did not have to cook on Christmas day. Afterwards he drove to his office, supposedly to pick up instructions from the home office. When he came back to the car, he said his instructions were to get his family out of Honolulu at once. We then drove directly to the pier by Aloha Tower where the ocean liner Lurline, still being reconfigured and painted grey for camouflage, was boarding. Dad took our suitcases, which were conveniently in the trunk (one per person), and boarded the ship. We were headed to the mainland, we knew not where.

As we pulled away from the dock, we waved to Dad on shore. He was being left behind. Would we ever see him again?

# V

My parents had made the decision—they had chosen to evacuate. If we stayed, and the Japanese invaded, we could be killed in the attack or suffer under occupation. Our friends in the Philippines were interned in Japanese prison camps for the duration of the war. If we left via convoy, we could be torpedoed and sunk in the Pacific. Small children did not stand much chance of survival when abandoning ship at sea. When my parents signed up for evacuation, they were instructed not to tell anyone and to have one suitcase per person packed and ready at all times. On Christmas Eve they had received the call. Between two and four o'clock Christmas afternoon we were to report to a ship docked near Aloha Tower. Perhaps we were sailing to safety, but Dad was being left behind on Hawaii. He was now manager of Kodak Hawaii and had to stay to help with the war effort by providing photographic services to the military.

We stood dejectedly on the deck. Several months earlier we had left Hawaii with a crowd of friends, leis and music. Now we were sneaking away in an effort to save our lives. Dad said this was the low point of his life. We never returned to our house, nor did Dad until over several months later. When he did return to the unlocked house, the Christmas tree was still up with pine needles and wrappings on the floor—nothing had been touched. His family had simply disappeared, and he now lived on a cot in his office. Mom was on a convoy with three young children sailing to an unknown destination with no support system ahead. Bob had lost his Felisa and now his father. He needed to be more mature than his years would allow. Bruce and I simply had to deal with the fears of war—and Bruce seemed to find the convoy thrilling. I clutched my doll more closely.

We were on the SS Lurline which had been converted into a troop carrier. Our convoy was comprised of three fast passenger ships and ten defensive vessels which could cruise at about 20 knots. In his book *Been There—Done That*[*] Bruce wrote:

> *A submerged submarine travelled at 7 to 10 knots. A fast convoy need fear only submarines lucky enough to be in front of the zigzagging convoy. Post-war intelligence tells us that five Japanese submarines were stationed near Pearl Harbor. One was sunk by aircraft on December 10th, so four were still near Pearl Harbor when we left on December 25th.*

Post-war intelligence is inconsistent on the actual number of submarines in the area but, regardless of the count, we moved in radio silence, blacked out at night. The entire convoy changed direction frequently and simultaneously, crisscrossing the Pacific to an unknown port. Lookout was constant and there was occasional gun practice. An American submarine accompanied us briefly on the surface, so everyone could see how a real submarine would appear in case we spotted one.

The ship was overcrowded with some wounded from Pearl Harbor, refugees like us and returning tourists. We were assigned to a cabin on E deck, far from the stairs. All the beds had been removed and replaced with cots or bunks to accommodate more people. In an emergency we were told all

---

[*] Gordon, Bruce E. *Been There—Done That, Adventures from 1934 to 2001.* 2001

lights would be switched off. Mom decided to move her family up to the promenade deck near our assigned lifeboat. She took our mattresses and put them under a ping-pong table.

Two meals a day were served cafeteria style and passengers stood in line for hours but there was nothing else to do. There were extra toilet facilities built on deck and bunks with cots in the swimming pool. There were *abandon ship* drills every day. We learned how to jump from the ship with our arms on top of our life jackets to prevent the cork floats from striking our jaws and breaking our necks. They told us how to splash away the burning oil which would cover the water. We wore our life jackets at all times except when we slept with them as our pillows.

As we sailed north, we became bone chillingly cold despite some blankets at night. They had stored all the suitcases in the hold, so we had only what we were wearing when we boarded the ship which was tropical clothing. Our move to the promenade deck close to our assigned lifeboat was subject to wind and salt air, making us even colder. Our clothes went unwashed for a week and the adults referred to their garments as being battleship grey. Life was difficult, but we were alive and relatively well.

Mom complimented us on being troopers—which meant we were dealing with the situation and not complaining. How could we complain when others were so much worse off? Where were our good friends in Manila, the Nashes? We later learned the Japanese occupied Manila on January 2nd and the Nashes were sent to Santo Tomas prison camp. Their family barely survived three years of hunger and captivity. We were the lucky ones.

The third day out was the most fearsome for the adults. If we were torpedoed, help would be unavailable in time from either the West coast or Hawaii. Mom tied us together by our life jackets because she didn't want to lose any one of us. We would perish, or survive, together. During an abandon ship drill as we rushed to our assigned lifeboat, a sailor tripped over our ropes. He yelled at Mom, "God damn it lady, untie your children!" Later it became something of a family joke but at the time it wasn't funny at all. None of the passengers knew where the ship would land. The ocean was so vast it seemed the whole convoy could sink and no one would know—the world would simply go on without us.

On January 1st, 1942, an airplane flew over us—and then another—and soon we could see land. Then we saw the Golden Gate Bridge in the distance. A crowd of people were lined up on the bridge waving to us. The whole ship was terribly relieved and joined in singing:

*San Francisco here I come, right back where I started from...*
*Open up that Golden Gate, California here I come.*

We sailed into the harbor on New Year's Day. The Red Cross met our ship, gave us warm clothes, made sure we had immediate necessities and took us to a hotel. It was a relief to exchange our beautiful Hawaiian light weight Christmas clothes for the ill-fitting warm flannel ones. In gratitude we have continued to donate to the Red Cross ever since. Eleanor Breed, Mom's friend from Beijing, came to the hotel to meet us. She worked for the San Francisco Chronicle and their photographer took a picture of our family for the paper, refugees from Pearl Harbor.

Before we left Hawaii, Dad and Mom had examined a map of the United States and chosen Tucson, Arizona, as our ultimate destination. Mom's parents had died the year before and so had Dad's mother so there was little reason to go to Rochester. A strong reason not to go was that Crawford, Mom's difficult brother, was still there, and she had been trying to avoid him for years. The North was too cold, the

East too far away from Hawaii, the West coast too vulnerable to invasion, so Tucson, Arizona, it was. As soon as possible we were on a train south. The railway tickets cost almost all the cash Mom had, so she arrived in Tucson with little money and three exhausted children. It was midnight when the train dumped us on the largely empty train platform. A taxi driver drove us to a hotel where the night clerk gave us a room without asking for money.

First thing the next morning Mom marched into the nearest bank.

"I would like to cash a check," she said.

"Is it from our bank?" asked the teller.

"No."

"On what bank?"

"The Bank of Hawaii."

"Is it a cashier's check?"

"No. A personal check."

"Do you know anyone here who can vouch for you?"

"No."

"Have you just arrived from Hawaii?"

"Yes."

"We would be happy to cash your check."

It was not the first or the last time in our lives we have found people willing to help those in difficult situations.

Now we needed inexpensive housing near a school. Mom quickly found a house to rent near the Sam Hughes Elementary School. Learning our situation, the school took the boys immediately. She returned to the hotel with me utterly exhausted. I have myself been a mother traveling with three young children and I find it amazing she accomplished all this so rapidly, but she had to—there was no choice. She had to be a trooper. But the stress was accumulating.

Anti-Japanese feeling was at a feverish pitch along the whole west coast. As in Hawaii, there had been an immediate roundup of Japanese the government considered suspicious but on the mainland it was followed up with internment for all Japanese. In Berkeley, California, Eleanor Breed's church helped with the evacuation of the Japanese-Americans in her area. In San Diego her sister Clara gained renown for her support of Japanese-American children from the city who were sent to relocation centers. The Japanese were told the public feared they were enemy agents and they were being interned for their own safety.

## In May 1942 the Philippines surrendered; we were losing the war

We liked Tucson. The boys could bicycle around by themselves (Bruce learned to ride there) and they loved to explore the desert. I often rode in a basket on Mom's bike. One rainy day Bruce went home from school for what he thought was an appointment, stood outside in the rain waiting for Mom who did not appear, went back to school and sat in wet clothes all afternoon. By nightfall he had a terrible earache and eventually he was hospitalized with pneumonia. Penicillin was not available to the public, so he was put in an oxygen tent and given sulfa drugs. Eventually he recovered, but it was his third brush with death in his short lifetime.

Mom worried about our landlord who seemed to pay too much attention to her and made her uncomfortable. Often it was so hot at night we would sleep outdoors, and he seemed to come by much too often. Furthermore, prices in the area were rising because Tucson was the site of Davis Monthan Airfield, and it was booming due to the war effort. When our rent doubled in just a few months, Mom and Dad corresponded about the possibility of our moving to Mexico where prices would be lower, and we could all learn Spanish. In September 1942 we moved to Guadalajara, Mexico. It was almost a tragedy.

The boys started in a Spanish-speaking school with little knowledge of Spanish—a difficult situation although a sympathetic teacher tried to help them. An amah took care of me. Poverty surrounded us. When we were in Manila, I had been a baby and unaware of poverty so conditions in Guadalajara shocked me. Even my mother, who remembered Manila well, felt the poverty in Mexico was much worse. I distinctly remember watching a ragged boy pick up a half-eaten sandwich out of a gutter and gulp it down hungrily. I imagined myself having to scrounge for food and the idea terrified me. To this day I have a deep sense of gratitude and good fortune for all the benefits I have had in my life, particularly food and shelter.

**In June 1942 America won the Battle of Midway and stopped the Japanese advance**

Soon we all became sick, but Bruce's intestinal upsets were the worst with diarrhea, vomiting and weakness to the point where he could barely walk. The toilets in our hotel only worked half the time. The stench did not help our digestive systems. Mom considered going back to the States, but she dreaded having to care for three children with no help. At least in Mexico servants were inexpensive. Finally, after going to several doctors who all prescribed the same medicine for Bruce, an American doctor in our hotel said to Mom, "I don't know what is wrong with Bruce, but he is dying. You must take him back to America." Mom packed us up, and we started on a nightmare trip by train up the west coast of Mexico back to Tucson.

Dad tells this story in his book *Milly*:

> *Their car was not air-conditioned and was slow. Milly felt she wanted to get out and push. At Santa Ana,*

a hundred miles or so from the U.S. border, a bridge had been weakened by flooding, and the train balked. There was no hotel and no restaurant, and the little tienda (store) selling vegetables had little she could use without cooking. By day their seats in the train were stifling hot and cold by night. Water was hot and in short supply. Milly was frantic. Eventually the passengers walked across the bridge and the train slowly followed.

Milly breathed a sigh of relief when they reached the American border at Nogales. Now she was only an hour from Tucson, but she had overlooked the U.S. Immigration Service. There were reports of German spies entering the U.S. from Mexico and, with a war on, Immigration was wary of disguises. All U.S. $20 bills were suspected of having been smuggled from Germany, and Milly had two of them. Immigration asked where she was born.

"Rochester, New York," she said.

"Were the children born there?" the office asked.

"No. They were born in the Philippines."

"What was your maiden name?"'

"Mildred Gleichauf."

"German. Sit down over there please."

Milly hadn't needed a passport and the papers she had were Mexican. Nothing would convince officials to let her go. Ann began to cry, and the boys were restless. The train whistled, and Milly was desperate.

Calling Sonny, then ten years old, she instructed him to get the family on the train and in Tucson to take a taxi to the Pioneer Hotel. Living there was an elderly couple, friends she knew, and he was to ask "Goatie" to get Bruce to a hospital as soon as possible. The children went off without her.

Bob remembers this as the scariest moment of his childhood. He was only nine years old (Dad's report was off a little) and in charge of a dying brother and a young crying sister. Bruce vomited on the floor of the railroad station and was so sick he could barely walk but made it to the train. When we reboarded, a lady passenger put her hand on Bob's shoulder and reassured him everything would be all right, a supporting gesture he still remembers. I was so shaken by the experience that many years later, when I visited the Nogales border with my husband, Tom, some border guards with a German shepherd dog came towards us and I panicked, running back to our car and sitting there sobbing. Tom didn't know what had happened, but I did—I was reliving our border crossing from long ago. As for Mom—I can hardly imagine what she was going through. She was sending all three of her children off alone, one of whom was critically ill. But Bruce's life was at stake.

Fortunately, the guards released Mom, and she boarded the end of the train—we never learned why they let her go. Walking up through the cars she reached her children and collapsed in our arms. We hugged each other desperately. In Tucson the Hofstadters helped get Bruce into a hospital where he slowly recovered from what the doctors told Mom was strychnine poisoning. Evidently when she increased the medication the Mexican physicians had given her because he did not improve, the medication itself had gradually been poisoning him. Mom felt guilty. Bruce now had a liver problem and was jaundiced. He weighed only forty-two pounds and was eight years old. Mom overheard the nurses say Bruce was dying. She was so upset she threw up and collapsed. The doctor smelled liquor on her breath and berated her for not disciplining herself. She was not an alcoholic but may have been drinking to seek relief from a great deal of stress. The doctor was not sympathetic.

This time it was much harder for Mom to find lodgings. Our first house had rented for $36 per month and gone up to

$75 per month during the few months we were there. Now a comparable house rented for $200 per month. Fortunately, her friends opened their homes. Bob went to stay at a friend's house, Bruce was in the hospital and then a nursing home, and another family offered to take me. At some point during this period, I started whining. Mom was very clear-troopers do not whine! Mom decided to keep me as long as she could. Eventually she found a house. She had to rely on Bob quite a lot for babysitting and shopping and, to some extent, companionship. Amidst all this stress, Mom wrote the following note to Dad:

> *In fact I'm getting from life exactly what I wanted, only*
> *I didn't realize it would cost so much or be so painful,*
> *but the results are soul satisfying and deep. I'd rather*
> *pay a hospital bill for Bruce than buy a mink coat!*

When he was well enough, Bruce came home. He continued to subsist on a diet of crackers and honey. Being bed-ridden so much he played mostly with airplanes, pretending he was shooting down Japanese Zeroes. We had a family tradition in the air as Dad was related to the Wright Brothers and Uncle Ray had been in naval aviation in WWI. Bruce was an avid reader and adventure books appealed to him, particularly those concerning flying.

Mom relied quite a bit on Bob. At Christmas she was so exhausted she gave Bob some money and a list of children whose parents had helped her a great deal. He did the purchasing, wrapping, labeling, and delivery too.

**In January 1943 the Russians stopped the Germans at Stalingrad**

Then we all got scarlet fever and were quarantined with a red sign on our house. Mother would bathe us with cold rags to get our temperatures down. Bob remembers being delirious. This time penicillin was available, and it aided our recovery. While the boys were still in bed, Bob threw a baseball through a short hall to Bruce, but missed, breaking a window—as if Mom did not already have enough problems. It was a great relief to Mom when we were all able to go back to school.

**In February 1943 Americans won the battle of Guadalcanal; the Pacific war was turning in America's favor**

By late spring Dad considered Honolulu safe enough to bring his family back to Hawaii. In July he secured passage to San Francisco on one of the last flights of the flying boats called Clippers, picked up Mom and me in Tucson, put the boys in the Greenfield School summer camp and headed to the home office. The boys loved Greenfield where they learned camp skills and how to identify enemy aircraft.

Dad, Mom and I took the train to Rochester. Standing on the platform at the end of the caboose with me in his arms, Dad commented on how the tracks came together in the distance. I laughed at him, "What is it, Daddy? An optical illusion?" I was only five and two school teachers near us on the platform were amazed. I was getting a reputation as the smart one and Bruce as the crack shot. Bob, whom Bruce and I admired tremendously, began to feel he was just average and to be a little jealous of his younger siblings. He became protective of his position as the oldest son.

In Rochester we saw friends and relatives and Dad spent time in the main office. Then we returned to Tucson, picked up the boys, and proceeded to San Francisco where we expected to find a ship back to Hawaii. Dad had essential work priority due to his role in the processing of military photography as manager of Kodak Hawaii. Within two days he booked passage on a freighter returning to Honolulu. Dad did not tell us in advance that he was leaving without us. Bob felt abandoned when Dad simply got in a taxi and left. As after Pearl Harbor, our parents were prohibited from discussing departures for security reasons. We had no priority and had to wait and wait, for nine months.

At first we stayed in the Canterbury Hotel. Mom enrolled Bruce and Bob in Redding Grammar school, within walking distance of the hotel. Soon Mom became sick and was hospitalized. Bruce says she thought she might have cancer because her father died of cancer, but we don't really know what ailed her. What could she do with the kids? Bob and Bruce stayed in the hotel. A Jewish woman named Mrs. D'Acre took care of the boys when they weren't at school. She even helped them celebrate Christmas by constructing a Christmas tree on the hotel wall with various decorations. Sometimes Eleanor Breed, Mom's friend from Beijing, took them hiking around Berkeley where she lived.

Mom sent me to stay with the Pyes, a couple with no children. The husband worked for Kodak in San Francisco. They lived in Oakland across the bay and enrolled me in school there. This period was particularly tough for me—a five then six-year-old in an unfamiliar place with strange people and no family. I was very lonely. But I was expected to be a trooper. Would I ever be reclaimed? The Pyes treated me well but were strict about eating. It is possible I had rheumatic fever at this time, following my bout of scarlet fever in Tucson. Sometimes one leads to the other, and I clearly was small and thin for my age. Years later doctors found I had a heart murmur, a common result of rheumatic fever. To build me up, the Pyes insisted I clean my plate every night. I remember sitting alone at their dining room table in the dark for what seemed like forever trying to finish my dinner.

Mom reported the Pyes were proud of me because I did

well in school although I am not sure what this means when you are so young. My experience in Oakland may have been the start of the confusion over my correct grade. My birthdate was January 7th, 1938, and schools differed on their cutoff dates for enrolling students.

When Mom returned to the hotel from the hospital, the boys got in trouble by throwing pebbles down from the roof and the manager wanted to expel them. There was nowhere else for them to go in wartime San Francisco, so he relented. Then Bob and Bruce became sick. Mom called a doctor. He concluded they were contagious.

"The boys will have to be quarantined," said the doctor.

"The hotel is not allowed to have quarantined residents," replied Mom.

"Then you will have to move," he suggested.

"No hotel will permit quarantined patients." said Mom.

"Then they will have to stay in your rooms," replied the doctor. "I will not report it to the management. I have never been here. Do not call me again."

And the doctor left.

Mom told the management the boys had colds and would stay in their rooms. I suspect this was good news for the management as the boys were often in trouble.

Finally, Mom received the anticipated telephone call regarding passage to Hawaii. She picked me up, packed our bags, and we took a taxi to the dock. On April 4th, 1944, we sailed out of San Francisco. We had survived life-threatening illnesses and separation and were heading back to Hawaii to reunite with Dad.

# VI

The merchant marine ship in which we traveled segregated the sexes. Mom and I bunked in the aft compartments with the women and Bruce and Bob in the front hold with the men. We saw each other in the middle of the ship on free time and at meals. Mom tried to continue our education while aboard ship. Bob remembers learning to calculate fractions on this trip by finding the common denominator. He usually did well in math and art but felt threatened by Bruce's ability at marksmanship and reading and my success in school. He began to think he was only average whereas, when we were younger, he was always best at everything.

Bruce described the return convoy as extremely difficult with four tier bunks and cursing, seasick men. Often sailors would whittle and talk. The boys started to whittle too, but then began throwing their knives into the deck trying to hit targets. Of course, the sailors stopped this sport due to damage to the deck. Bob had a bet with another boy and, when he thought no one was looking, threw his knife into the deck. Suddenly a sailor grabbed him by the hair, confiscated his knife and told him he had better behave or else! He could retrieve his knife by asking the Captain for it and explaining why it was taken away. He did not go to the Captain.

Another time Bob got into a fight and was hit in the face. He chased the other boy around the deck, caught him, and slugged him. A woman yelled, and a sailor pulled them apart. The woman said it was all Bob's fault—he started it. All she had seen was Bob chasing the boy and slugging him. As usual, Bob considered his punishment unfair.

Mom and I had a less stressful voyage but, as we prepared for our arrival, I feared I would not recognize my father. I am not sure why I felt this way. It had only been nine months since I had last seen him. Later I learned Bruce, too, feared he might not recognize Dad. As we pulled into the pier, however, there was Dad on the dock and we ran down to hug him.

After we left Honolulu on December 25th, 1941, Dad had moved into his office. He ate and slept there for three months with other Kodak employees. At night they took turns patrolling the building. There were frequent air raid sirens, most of them due to friendly planes. Dad's pre-war Intelligence clearance for the Navy came in handy as the office developed films of the Pearl Harbor attack and the Doolittle raid on Tokyo.

Three months later they were no longer required to patrol the building at night, so Dad moved back to our house in Wailupe with several other Kodak employees who were temporarily bachelors. However, he soon received an offer to purchase the house and sold it, moving into a hotel to await our return. The Kodak staff, about one hundred before the attack, dropped to fifty, and then rose to two hundred as they processed V-mail (photographs of mail) and preformed other military work.

Dad found a house for us on Makiki Heights on Mount Tantalus. It overlooked the city and Mom put in a large picture window to take advantage of the view. We had a bomb shelter and received gas masks. One night when the air raid sirens blared we crowded into the shelter and found it full of spiders and mosquitoes. Fortunately, the alarm was false, and we didn't have to stay underground for long.

There were many wartime restrictions. Car headlights were painted black with just a small hole to emit a little light. Private cars were not manufactured during the war because of military priority, so we bought an old car with a rumble seat. Gas remained rationed. Big tape strips made X marks on large windows to reduce the shattering of glass by explosions.

Everyone helped with the war effort. Mom volunteered as a Grey Lady with the Red Cross, taking care of soldiers in Tripler Army Hospital. She found the burn victims particularly upsetting. As she was prone to depression and headaches, I am amazed she continued to work there. We all had war projects with the Cub Scouts, Boy Scouts or Brownies and Dad's office, of course, continued to process film and v-mail for the Army and Navy.

## The Japanese surrendered to the Allies on September 2nd, 1945

Our Christmas card photo that year showed us moving out of our bomb shelter. Shortly after the picture was taken, it was demolished. It was now peacetime. I enrolled in Hanahauoli School and the boys in Punahou School. Their classes were still being held at the University of Hawaii Teachers College. The Army Corps of Engineers had commandeered the Punahou campus on December 8th, 1941. On September 10, 1945, the older Punahou students marched en masse from the University of Hawaii to reoccupy the Punahou campus. Bob has always felt very attached to Punahou and has stayed in touch with some of his friends from this era. As soon as I was old enough, I joined the boys at Punahou.

Hawaii was a child's paradise. We went barefoot almost all the time except on Sundays to church. We slid down the grassy slope adjoining our house on homemade sleds or Ti leaves. We hiked in the halikoa. We played softball and touch football. We spent as little time as possible indoors. Bruce enjoyed watching the Navy tow target barges past the big coastal guns on Koko Head mountain. He would see the puff of smoke from the gun, wait for the sound of the boom; then see the spout of water somewhere around the target barge. Bruce never saw one hit its target. His eyesight was excellent; mine was almost as good. We competed against each other at identifying the names of ships in the distance.

The neighborhood boys talked about a bomb crater near to our house and one day they took Bob and Bruce up to see it. On March 4th, 1942, two Japanese planes had flown over the island to observe and bomb the repair facilities at Pearl Harbor. As the city was in blackout and there was fog over their target, they could not find their way and dropped their bombs randomly. One of them landed and exploded within a mile of our house and the other next to Roosevelt school. At that time we were on the mainland. This was called the second Pearl Harbor attack, but it was small and unsuccessful. However, it spurred an investigation into where the planes originated. They had flown from the Marshall Islands to French Frigate Sholes and then on to Honolulu. American naval forces were sent to patrol the area around the Sholes to prevent further use of this route. Inability to refuel caused the Japanese to cancel subsequent observational sorties over Pearl, thus discouraging further attacks on American forces in Honolulu.

About this time, I discovered the advantages of being the youngest and the only girl. Bob was my idol; Bruce was my target. I found I could easily blame him for lots of things and Mom believed me. He remembers smashing the head of my doll to find out how the eyes worked. I remember wanting to know how the eyes worked (and how it cried from its chest). Bruce got in trouble for breaking my doll and remembers he did it. Maybe he did—it is not clear. I certainly know I was as interested as he was. Maybe I did. Sometimes I would tattle on him just because I wasn't getting what I wanted. As adults,

I have apologized to him and we are good friends, but I was a difficult little sister to Bruce.

The boys pulled a trick on the young Army Intelligence officer who rented a room on the lower floor of our house.. Bob wrote a note in French about spies meeting in a hideout in the woods. They drew a rough map with an X showing the rendezvous place—a lava cave nearby. They left the note where the Lieutenant would find it and he did—resulting in a military search of the area which found the cave with evidence of human activity but no spies. Mom was exasperated by the boys' continuous pranks and took them to a psychiatrist. He examined them, then simply advised her to put a sign at the end of her bed: "This phase will pass." Taking care of children was harder than she expected.

Another project of Bruce's involved preserving flies. He read about how wooly mammoths stayed frozen in the ground for a long time without decaying. He was deadly with a fly swatter so he killed some flies and put them in an ice cube tray in the refrigerator. Unfortunately Mom had a dinner party with cocktails. There were dead flies floating in the drinks.

Birthday parties seemed to depend on how much help Mom had. She had little help during this time in Honolulu. One year she seemed to have forgotten my birthday. I decided to buy her a present with the selfish idea it would remind her it was my birthday. It worked, and I did get a present, but no party. I don't remember any of us having birthday parties during this period in Honolulu. When my children were growing up, I gave them a party every year until they reached twelve although my parties were never as creative as hers.

Mom's mother, who died in 1940, left what little she had to her four children. However, Mom's brother Ray urged them to give everything to their father who was critically ill and low on funds, and Mom did. Her father died a few months later, and he left everything to Crawford because her father believed Crawford needed it more than his siblings. Aunt Matie had set aside grandma's silver tea service for Mom because her mother had promised it to her. Matie gave it to Mom on her next visit. The silver had been her mother's 25th anniversary present. When Crawford found out he sent a letter to Dad claiming Mom had stolen it and must return the tea service to him or he would get his lawyers after her. Dad was furious but had her pack it up and send it to Crawford with a courteous note explaining she understood her mother had intended it for her—but since it was his, she was returning it. There wasn't enough postage on the package so Crawford sent a letter back insisting they pay the postage due. They did. Crawford then sold the silver for cash. Dad swore he would NEVER do anything more for Crawford. A few years later when he was in Washington, D.C., Dad purchased a lovely tea service for Mom but it could not heal the wound.

During this stay in Honolulu I fell in love with sports. I was becoming tougher. When one was pinned down, you would be released if you said "*Uncle.*" I would bawl my eyes out but I wouldn't say "*Uncle.*" Finally the boys would let me go. Bob and Bruce took judo lessons and trained me to yell "sa toh" as I landed so they could use me for practice. They played pickup softball and touch football and I tagged along. I was the last chosen for every team, but I was delighted to play at all. In touch football I would be placed way in the backfield and sometimes was the only person between the ball carrier and the goal. When I caught him, I felt like a hero. I was referred to as *Me Too*, much as Bruce had been, because I always wanted to join the games.

It turned out I am ambidextrous and left—eyed. This was an advantage in many sports but a bit confusing for me as I kept switching arms and feet. After a while I simply did some things right handed and some left-handed, as well as switching feet when kicking or running. As an adult I have continued to use both sides, playing golf right handed but putting left handed and using a left handed seven iron under trees. Usually if someone taught me how to play something, I do it right handed, but if I learned by myself, I do it left handed. Years later I had two daughters, one right handed and one left handed.

Punahou had some special traditions. We were mostly barefoot in the elementary grades—shoes were not required until the upper grades. We had lessons in hula, ukulele, typing and, of course, everyone had to be able to swim. The younger students took naps in school every day on straw mats. We loved the old childhood games such as jumping rope and marbles. One of our neighbors was Martha Cook Derby. She was a descendent of one of the original missionary founders of the Honolulu community. She had a German Shepherd dog, Nahi, who bit me once and also, on other occasions, bit both my brothers. The Derbys later moved Nahi to their farm on Molokai, an outer island less populated than Oahu, to reduce his contact with people. Although I like dogs, and we usually had at least one, I was bitten by dogs three times, all German Shepherds, so I stay away from them, even as an adult. They are very loyal to their owners but sometimes a threat to others.

One summer Martha invited me to spend time with her family on Molokai, which I did. We went horseback riding and swimming almost every day. They had cream for breakfast so thick we used it as butter on pancakes—absolutely delicious. I was very blond and kept my hair in a braid so it wouldn't get in my eyes when I was swimming. Daily chlorinated water from their pool dripped down the braid. Eventually the end of the braid turned greenish. When I came back to Honolulu Mom cut off all the green hair, and I sported a new short bob. I later learned it wasn't the chlorine itself which turned my hair green but the copper in the water reacting with the chlorine.

As a child I found it almost impossible to make long-term friends as we moved so much. I have been able to stay in touch, however, with Martha Derby and Janie Ogawa, my friend from before the war in Wailupe and later again at Punahou. The Ogawas still lived in Wailupe after the war. When a tsunami hit Hawaii on April 1st, 1946, they escaped injury but there was considerable damage to the property of those who lived along the beach.

Mom was never much of a cook although she loved dinner parties and set an elegant table. She had little experience cooking before she was married—and then they had cooks in Chile and Manila. When she did cook for company, she gave it her all. One of her specialties was cinnamon rolls. They took two days to make because the yeast had to rise. One day when we were entertaining company outside on the lawn, Bruce carried the freshly baked rolls to where we gathered. He couldn't resist pretending to be a waiter and showing off by holding one tray up in each hand. Walking downhill on grass, he began to slip. He grabbed at the tray in his right hand with his left hand—and all the rolls went flying. Coming out of the kitchen, Mom was practically in tears. Now it seems funny, but then it was serious. Poor Bruce!

Mom showed her emotions on the surface more than Dad. One time she made a soufflé, a dish with cheese and eggs. A soufflé rises and must be eaten as soon as cooked or it will collapse. Dad was working on a project using his tools and never left a job without putting things away. When Mom called "Dinner's ready" he took his time and put all the tools away before going up to dinner. By the time he arrived the soufflé had fallen. Mom was mad and said so. Dad simply left the table and went for a walk—he would not allow himself to lose his temper, at least in front of his children. We never had soufflé again.

As many siblings do, we had individual roles within the family. Bob was the leader whom Bruce and I admired. Our parents expected him to grow up to be a lawyer or some other professional. In writing about himself years later, however, Bob described himself as having no talents and little confidence—not the picture we had of him. He had an open, warm personality and made friends easily, but I began to understand he did not often think about the other side of issues or how other people felt. He simply knew they were wrong, and he was right. A playmate, Malcolm Ing, hit Bruce "in the face without warning and without cause. I could not let this act of violence be left unpunished" he wrote. So Bob protected his brother by having a challenge fist fight with Malcolm. Bruce didn't feel it necessary, but Bob did. He saw the world in black and white. I saw it as gray. Both Bob and Dad had strong moral compasses. They both had tempers although Dad kept his under control with more success than Bob.

Bruce loved the outdoors and Mom and Dad thought he should be a farmer. He was usually messy and often responsible for accidents. When something went wrong, we would all yell "Bruce" because time and again it was his fault. He liked to read and was frequently engrossed in reading about someone else's outdoor adventures. He remained calmer under pressure than Bob and looked at issues more practically and less abstractly than his brother. Bruce felt farming would not be right for him because it required expensive land and farm equipment, neither of which he would have. It would take time for him to find an occupation which suited him.

I was the youngest, a weakling and easily frightened, but the best student and the best athlete. As I was a girl, my parents expected I would get married and not need a career. My dreams were not of boys and marriage but of a career of my own. So I just lived day-to-day, gradually becoming physically and mentally stronger. My brothers called me a burnt marshmallow as I developed a thicker skin on the outside but was still soft on the inside. Dealing with fear required constant work. The world was a scary place.

When the war ended in 1945 the previous head of Kodak Hawaii, who had served as a naval officer during the war, returned and resumed his job. Dad accepted a temporary position with the Army Exchange Service with the standing of Major. He toured the Japanese WWII battle sites and took photographs for occupation troops. He brought back amazing pictures of Manila Bay filled with half-submerged ships and decrepit taxis running on coal in Japan. American servicemen were repatriated more rapidly than expected so the job ended. Then he accepted a temporary position heading the Kodak office in Manila. In March 1946 he became manager of Kodak China and moved to an office on the Bund in Shanghai.

Conditions in Shanghai were chaotic, but this was the most exciting and challenging time in Dad's career. Inflation was rampant and crime widespread. When Dad went to Rotary one day, he paid CNY2,000 at the beginning of lunch. The price rose CNY100 during lunch. By the time Dad left Shanghai three years later the exchange rate reached twelve million yuan to one US dollar, and it continued to climb. My parents thought of enclosing a CNY1,000,000 note with each Christmas card they sent that year, just for fun.

Safety was a major problem. Dad told the following story about one of his employees:

> *Going home in a Pedi cab late one night in January, he was robbed by the coolie who held a gun on him and demanded not only his wallet and overcoat but even his suit coat. He remonstrated because of the cold, and the coolie shot him, stripped the coat from him and hurried away. The young man crawled to*

*a nearby house and explained in Chinese that he was
an American and had been shot. Fortunately for him
he was taken to an American hospital...*

Besides inflation and safety, the Chinese way of *cum sha*, sometimes called kickbacks, continued unabated and caused its own problems. Sometimes one could be a beneficiary of it as when Mom had received *cum sha* for taking her friend shopping in Beijing many years earlier. In Shanghai local shopkeepers often put one of every item in the store in the front window, giving a very cluttered look. When new Kodak display materials arrived in Shanghai, Dad had his own employee set up a dealer's window with woodland scenes, fall colors and romping children. In passing the window a few days later he noticed the display was hidden behind a large cut-out of a competitor's camera. The shopkeeper explained: "Mistah Gordon, he pay me cash putee his piecee in window. How much you pay?"

His dealers found many ways to make a dollar. Dad found one of them selling his goods for the same price he bought them from Kodak. How could he make a profit? Case quantities in those days were shipped in large pine boxes lined with tar paper. The dealer's profit came from selling the boxes.

Business in Shanghai proceeded well at first but then fell off due to increasing disruption from the Nationalist-Communist conflict. Dad hesitated to bring his family there. One night a woman and her child outside the hotel where Dad stayed were crying because they were freezing to death. The establishment would not take them in because of the riot it would cause—there were so many others in the same situation they would mob the hotel. Mom had fond memories of Shanghai and could hardly believe these reports. In October she left us in Honolulu with a caretaker and flew out to visit Dad and see for herself. Housing was scarce and very expensive due to war damages. The Chinese government had frozen rents, so instead of raising rents, one paid *key money*, a onetime payment to gain access to the apartment or house. Key money for an acceptable apartment or house could be twice Dad's annual salary with no receipt given. He appealed to the home office for help, but they would not agree to the conditions. Hong Kong was more stable than Shanghai and gradually became more profitable. Dad decided to move his family to Hong Kong. Mom sold our house in Honolulu and in 1947 Dad flew there, picked us up, and we all traveled on to the United States. I was sorry to be leaving my friends in Hawaii but looking forward to a new adventure.

As usual, we did not go directly to Rochester but stopped to sightsee along the way. In New Mexico we saw the Carlsbad Caverns, an experience I found awe-inspiring. In Rochester we stayed briefly with Laura Barker's family. She was Dad's sister and we all liked her kids. They were explorers as we were. Billy Barker showed Bruce how to burn sulphur and capture the smoke in an empty jar. Bruce put the mayonnaise jar in their refrigerator to cool it down so the smoke would clear. Laura saw the empty jar, took it out and opened it, releasing the awful smell. It was just one more of Bruce's experiments with disturbing consequences.

In preparation for the trip to China I received an inoculation in my butt with what turned out to be a rusty needle. In those years hypodermic needles were often reused. It broke off inside me and had to be removed with minor surgery. I could barely sit down for a few days. But we had all been trained to be troopers.

Dad got into an argument on top of the Empire State building when he tried to take a picture of his family and a professional photographer asked him to move. Dad had been standing there first but it was the spot the professional photographer normally used. The argument embarrassed all of us but particularly Bob. To me it reflected both Dad and Bob's tendencies to stand up for their positions because they knew they were right. Dad usually controlled his anger better than Bob and could walk away whereas Bob would get into a fight. Perhaps Dad reacted so strongly this time because he was with his family. It was a minor incident but we all remember it because it was so unusual.

We picked up a Mercury convertible and drove across the country, visiting relatives and friends as we went. In Chicago Mom met with Grace Nash, her close friend from Manila who had spent the war in Japanese prison camps. In the Dakotas, Bob spied a bus of boys from Punahou. He wanted to join them and Dad said yes—we would reconnect in Yellowstone. Bob loved being with his Punahou friends but one of the boys had the mumps. By the time he rejoined us in Yellowstone, Bob had been exposed to them. A wonderful week at a dude ranch in Kalispell, Montana followed, but just as it ended Bob came down with the mumps. He doesn't remember much more of this trip because he became sick and delirious. I, however, remember well getting out of the car in Glacier National Park to play in the icy snow on the side of the road. Soon my feet hurt so much I was on the verge of tears. Mom soon realized my feet were wet and very cold in my sneakers even though it was a warm day in the summer. I had never been in snow before and did not recognize the sensation.

This time the whole family was able to fly to Hong Kong. Mom still had motion sickness, but at least the trip was much shorter than by steamer. While Bob was recovering from the mumps, Bruce came down with them shortly before we arrived in Hong Kong. He had to hide his swollen neck from immigration authorities in Hong Kong by wrapping a scarf around his neck in hot weather. No one noticed. I am always afraid of Immigration officials. We always seemed to have some potential problem—paper work, health etc.—and I was prone to speak out when it was most important to keep my mouth shut. On this occasion I managed to keep quiet and was proud of myself.

Dad plays football
at the University of Rochester

Dad in Manila

Mom in Beijing

Mom and Prince
Purachatra of Siam

Arrival in Chile

In Chile after Anne Hathaway

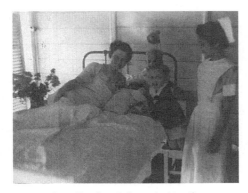

Ann Gordon is born in Manila

Family Christmas card 1938, Manila

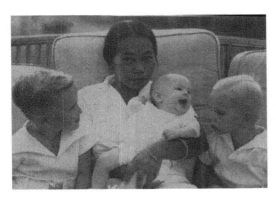

Children and Felisa

Kids at Haunama Bay, Oahu

Mom and Ann doing the hula

Family Christmas card 1941

December 7th, 1941 – Pearl Harbor

Refugees arrive in
San Francisco
(Red Cross clothes)

Guadalajara

Our WWII bomb shelter in Honolulu before demolition

All that remained of our house in Manila were the steps

Preparing for Hong Kong

Hong Kong
1948

Greetings from the Gordons

Off to schools (with Kitsue)

Tom Bain and Ann Gordon wedding 1959

# VII

The British chose the original site of the city of Hong Kong for its harbor, not its potential for an airfield. It included Hong Kong Island, with high peaks and a small fishing village on the waterfront, ceded to the British in 1842; Kowloon across the bay with some rather flat land and hills rising in the distance, ceded in 1860; and the New Territories, a large, hilly area stretching back to the current border, leased in 1898. As there was little level land on Hong Kong Island, the British built Kai Tak airport on Kowloon between low hills on one side and a mountain range on the other. Incoming planes swooped down sharply onto a short, narrow landing strip and outgoing flights rose precipitously to avoid crashing into the mountains.

In 1947 one held one's breath as your plane descended over the hills and buildings onto what one hoped would be a safe landing. We flew in only eight months after a Philippine Airlines DC-3 slammed into Mount Parker, killing all passengers and crew. One building below our flight path was Central British School which we later attended. Several years after our arrival, the airport added a landing strip out into Kowloon Harbor to accommodate larger planes, but it was still hazardous and accidents continued. Even that was not good enough, and eventually an entirely new airport, Chek Lap Kok, was constructed on an island not far from the city.

Exhausted from our long flight from Honolulu, we made our way by taxi along congested Waterloo Road to temporary accommodations in the Peninsula Hotel. Always color conscious, I noticed almost all the signs and advertisements had some red on them. Combined with the din of thousands of people going about their business and peddlers singing out their wares, it made an exciting scene. The hotel had served as Japanese military headquarters during World War II and had been strafed by Allied aircraft. Bullet holes remained in the facade. It had been the premier hotel in the colony and efforts were being made to take this position again. What could be done rapidly had been done. Repairing masonry would take some time. The waiters wore immaculately white uniforms, and the service was impeccable.

The Japanese had treated the population harshly during the war. So many Chinese had fled or been deported, the city had dropped from one and a half million people at the start of the conflict to five hundred thousand at the end. Today there are over seven million. The Japanese had commandeered everything they could find, producing scarcities in chickens, eggs and milk. One evening when we dined in the hotel they served us Baked Alaska—a dessert made with lots of egg whites. I could not understand how, with so few chickens left alive in the city, the hotel could serve Baked Alaska. Later, when taking a cooking class in school, I learned to cook with powdered milk and powdered eggs and realized the Baked Alaska had been made from powered egg whites.

Dad had purchased a lovely two-story Spanish-Colonial style granite house near the top of winding Ho Man Tin Hill road. There was a view overlooking the Kowloon peninsula on one side and towards Kai Tak airport in the distance on the other. At first Mom was disappointed by the poor condition of the house, which had been occupied by Japanese soldiers. For some unknown reason, a bathtub was sitting in what became the dining room.

Mom threw herself into repairing the damage. The house had parquet floors of imported oak but they were crisscrossed with multiple burn marks made by officers putting out their cigarettes. She hired a dozen coolies to sand them off but Dad, when he saw so many men at work, sent all but two of them home and rented an electric sander to finish the job. She installed an imported glass table and a chandelier in the dining room, and they were spectacular. This house became a wonderful setting for entertaining. All the rooms were spacious with high ceilings. The bathroom had French doors on three sides. It felt strange taking a bath in such a huge room without curtains or solid walls except on one end. There was a small lawn where we could play and often dine. The servants' quarters were in the back.

Mom had brought cases of home furnishings with us including silverware packed into the bottom of a carved Philippine chest. During the renovations, the house was robbed, but the thieves didn't look in the bottom drawer of the chest, and the silver remained. With the work completed, we had no problem with theft. The house had a tall stone wall all around, topped by shards of glass and concertina wire. Hong Kong, although much safer than Shanghai, was nevertheless filled with people barely surviving and robberies were common.

Hong Kong was the highlight of my childhood. Every day, every street, every person was different. Newness, while exciting, can be disconcerting. I enrolled in Kowloon Junior School and the boys in Central British School. My birthdate of January 7th was just after the start of the year. In Arizona and California the schools placed me ahead one-half year instead of behind a half year. Now in this British school their school year started in January, not September, and I moved up another half grade.

The first day in a new school was always difficult. This time, when I walked into class and the teacher introduced me to the other students, she asked me to go to the blackboard in front of the room and solve an addition problem with pounds, schillings and pence. I simply added them up. She assigned me to a seat at the extreme left front of the classroom. At lunch time I learned it was the dunce seat. I did not know you had to convert twelve pence to a shilling and twenty shillings to a pound—obviously I was well behind the rest of the class. Nor had I studied French which British schools did from the earliest grades. Most of the schools I attended enjoyed showing off how advanced they were compared to any previous school I had attended.

Mom's friend Eleanor Breed came to my rescue later in the day. She had given me a box of Tootsie rolls and bubble gum in San Francisco as a going away present. I distributed these to my new classmates. They were a tremendous treat to these students in a city just recovering from Japanese occupation, and I was not above buying friendship. I acquired the nickname "Bubbles." Chatting with my new friends, I walked down a flight of stairs and put my arm on the banister. Everyone gasped, and I soon learned why—I stuck to the banister. Hong Kong was so hot and humid varnish could remain sticky for a long time.

I learned an important moral lesson in Kowloon Junior School, but not the way it was intended. They distributed some yarn and needles so we could learn to knit. I was intrigued, so much so I *borrowed* the needles and yarn without asking and took them home to practice. Somehow, I never returned them—the longer I waited to return them the more difficult it seemed. This theft bothered me for years. It taught me doing things right in the first place was much easier than living with yourself when you did something wrong.

Eventually I moved up to Central British School which Bob and Bruce attended. The school building had served as a British military hospital just before the war, a Japanese hospital during the war, and then a British hospital again following the war. It was just getting back on its feet as a school when we were students there, permitting non-British students starting in 1947. It became one of the most respected schools in Hong Kong.

I was enrolled in the lowest grade, called Upper Remove. We had only one Chinese girl in my class and she was terrified of our huge male teacher. He had one deaf ear and would lean his deaf ear towards her and shout, "I can't hear you." The louder he shouted the softer her voice became. In fact, most of the students feared the teachers and did not ask questions. There were only a few Americans in the school and other students occasionally recruited us to ask questions for them because they were afraid and the Americans were not. We had come mostly from schools without corporal punishment.

Boys were taught mechanical drawing and shop; girls took a home economics class. We learned to cook with many substitutes. In school one day we made creamed cauliflower by first washing out most of the maggots (residue from night soil cultivation), boiling it (which killed the remaining maggots and sterilized the food), and then making a cream sauce with powdered milk and powdered eggs. Just the thought of the maggots made me unable to eat our finished product. There was a windowsill between the school hallway and the home economics room and, if we put our food there, passing boys always ate it. I put my creamed cauliflower on the windowsill.

At home our cook, Ah Kwan, was in charge of all the servants and their lodging. The head servant was referred to as the Number One Boy. He soon became head of the local Number One Boys Club partly because of how many eggs his family (us) ate. His wife, Ah Chung, was the laundress. We also had a succession of houseboys, the first of whom was Ah Key. When Ah Key left, Mom hired a new one. He did not have a servant's name. The "Ah" in front of servants' names in Cantonese showed he was a regular member of the household. Mom thought it would be fun to call him Ah Heck, and so it was.

Ah Kwan's wife did the washing by hand for some time but Mom wanted to buy her a washing machine and drier. Ah Chung was not pleased because she feared they might replace her, but she agreed to try. The first time she used the washer, it agitated violently. The load was unbalanced, and the machine not securely anchored. She thought it was chasing her around the room and screamed. Dad cut the power, and it stopped with a thud. She said: "I go wash-wash too, but I no go dance-dance!" A repair man came to balance the machine and put its feet into concrete pads so it couldn't move. Ah Chung became used to the machine and later, when it broke down, she kept asking when it would be repaired.

One-week Dad felt the rice bill was unusually high and went into the servant's quarters to discuss it with Ah Kwan. He found two men he did not know and asked who they were. Ah Kwan said they were his cousins from Foochow (Fuqing). As Dad watched the activity in the following months, he found our house was serving as an underground railway for immigrants trying to move to Hong Kong from Ah Kwan's native village. Dad kept an eye on the traffic but let it continue.

Across the street was a British family with two girls and down the side alley was a Chinese-English family with a boy named Tony Jenks. My brothers became friends with Tony, but I did not seem to bond with the British girls. Thanks to our parents I grew up practically color blind as far as race was concerned. I even had trouble in Hong Kong telling Chinese men from British men until I realized British men wore short pants (walking shorts). We had many parties at our house, and the ethnic issue could get hot. Both Tony and the girls came to one of our parties. When the girls found

Tony there, they left because they did not socialize with half-breeds. I was just appalled.

My mother, trying to be a good neighbor, went to the British home for tea one day and thanked the Chinese servant for serving her. Her hostess corrected her: "Milly dear, one doesn't thank the servants. They are paid to serve you." At first, I thought this attitude was just held by British colonialists but later I found some Americans acting the same way. On another occasion one of the British girls mentioned her father had accidentally killed someone in an automobile accident, but then she exclaimed "Oh, it didn't matter. He was only a Chinese." There were people who believed there were so many Chinese they did not value life as much as white people did.

Behind our house there was a steep slope down to a Chinese cemetery which was a place of special fascination for us. Following a Chinese funeral procession through the streets with mourners and firecrackers, bodies were taken to the cemetery where one could buy joss paper money for the afterlife. The paper money was burned so the smoke ascended to heaven to provide for the future needs of the deceased spirit. Sometimes the joss had pictures of necessary items and was buried with the deceased. Due to limited burial plots and the fact that many Hong Kong residents came from other villages, they sometimes buried bodies and then exhumed them after seven years. Cemetery workers scraped the bones and set them out to dry on mats. Once dry, the bones or cremated remains were placed in urns, taken to the ancestral burying grounds and reburied. During the Qingming period for honoring one's ancestors, one would see people lined up at the train station, urns in hand, heading back to the family ancestral site for reburial. The grave sites were then reused.

In the cemetery we found a Japanese helmet with a bullet hole in it—the wearer must have been killed. The helmet made a great prop when my brothers played war, Bruce's favorite activity. When he wrote about this time in Hong Kong, Bruce almost always mentioned something military. In our British school, he recited "The Midnight Ride of Paul Revere." He described the British battle against pirates in Bias Bay. He mentioned the smuggling in Macao and the crash of the PBY (seaplane). He reported finding a live hand grenade on a beach. In one way we were living in the same place, but in another, we weren't.

City water was restricted to certain hours of the day and expensive, so we provided our own water for sewage and the garden. We had a well and pump at the bottom of the hill behind our house. Someone stole the pump, so we replaced it in a concrete guard box with an iron gate. The gate was broken, and the pump stolen again. We installed a new gate and chained a book to the top where policemen signed to show they checked on the pump. The book was stolen.

One day a friend and I were walking along a winding, narrow path through the cemetery. Just ahead of me a snake slithered across the walkway. Recently the British family had found a king cobra nest with eggs on their property and Dad had shown me a picture of one. I knew a cobra when I saw one.

I froze.

"What's wrong?" my friend asked, bumping into me.

To move was impossible-I could only point. The cobra stopped, coiled a bit, raised its head, and spread its hood.

I could not speak and remained still.

Then the snake put down his head and continued across the path into the tall grass on the hill behind our house.

As soon as we got home I went inside, took our 22-caliber rifle, and went out to kill the snake. The hillside was a mix of wild grasses. I tried to keep my balance on the slope while watching out for the snake. It occurred to me the snake would find me before I found it. I would probably barely even see the strike—and how would I get the long rifle aimed in time, let alone hit a slithering, thin target. I realized how stupid my reaction was, went back into the house and put the gun away. I swore my friend to secrecy and told no one for years because I was so ashamed of not thinking clearly. I was becoming braver, but not smarter. There are different reactions to danger—some people pull back (me as a young child), some people attack (me as I matured) and some people have the presence of mind to stay calm and think (I never reached this stage, but I believe my brother Bruce did).

Discipline at school was strict. Girls were rapped on their palms with a ruler; boys, if the offense were grave, were caned. One day when his teacher left the room Bob got into a fight with Radar, the son of an American missionary. Just as the teacher came back into the room, they fell on a chair and broke it. The two boys were sent to the vice-principal's office for caning. The school had several bamboo canes, and a boy had to choose his own weapon of punishment. Bamboo can be whippy. When Bob got home and showed Dad the red stripes on his backside, Dad was furious, but Bob didn't want him to say anything to the school. Dad said he thought caning went out with Charles Dickens. Bob remembered there had been paddling in the Tucson public schools when we were there.

Now we had servants again, and Mom resumed giving special parties, both for their adult friends and for our friends. We had a Halloween party which became the talk of the town. There were still few Americans in the area and both the Chinese and British were unfamiliar with our Halloween rituals. They believed Americans could do almost anything. Mom set up the house with different activities in various rooms. The study was where Admiral Nelson's body lay. We reminded the blindfolded guests that Lord Nelson had lost his arm and eye at the Battle of Trafalgar before dying. Then we escorted them, one by one into Dad's study. First the child put his hand on what he believed was Nelson's cold chest (actually the chest of one of my brothers lying on a sofa covered with a clammy towel). Then he felt the stub of Nelson's amputated arm (just a folded arm) and finally we took his finger and jammed it into Nelson's eye (a hole in a soft orange). Most kids screamed and then couldn't wait to watch their friends go through it.

Another room supposedly had an airplane. We placed the blindfolded guest on the middle of an ironing board described as the cockpit of a small plane. My mom manned a vacuum cleaner.

My brothers cupped their mouths with their hands to create a muffled sound:

"CX4 to control tower. Ready on runway one."

"Control tower to CX4. Ready for takeoff."

Mom turned the vacuum cleaner on the blow setting so the child heard the motor and then she edged the breeze onto the face of the child.

Next the ironing board wobbled as my brothers lifted it into the air over a bed. In excited voices they blurted out:

"Trouble in engine one. Trouble in engine one."

"Abort! Abort!"

Hard shaking and then my brothers turned the ironing board over and dumped the child on the bed.

Again, fear and excitement. The guest could hardly wait to see the next child take his ride.

Mom's parties for adults were stunning. She set a magnificent table with crystal and china. She was doing what she really loved. Ah Kwan cooked and he and Ah Heck served, but she was in charge of the table setting and flowers. I don't remember her having headaches at this time.

One evening Bruce learned the dinner party guests were having meringues with strawberries and whipped cream for dessert. He asked Ah Kwan to bring one to his room and wake him up if there were any extra. Well, there was one.

The next morning at breakfast Bruce commented on how sorry he was there were no left-overs.

"Oh, little Master, there was one, and I gave it to you," said Ah Kwan.

"No, you didn't," Bruce replied.

He took Bruce into his room and there, sitting next to his bed, was the empty plate. Bruce had eaten the delicious dessert and could not remember it. He was devastated.

Breakfast was my favorite meal not only because I like breakfast food but also because I liked watching my father's hair. He was slightly above average height for his era with curly brown hair he kept short because curls were considered effeminate. In the morning he would shower and comb his hair flat. At breakfast it would slowly dry, popping up into curls as it did so. I found it very entertaining.

We had a tradition in our family: if someone at the dinner table asked for something right next to him, he had to stand up, bow three times and repeat:

"The sugar was right near me.

"The sugar was right near me.

"The sugar was right near me."

One day Dad was not paying attention and asked for the salt, which was right next to his glass. At our insistence he got up, bowed three times and repeated: "The salt was right near me…"

Ah Kwan was dismayed. The head of the house should not do this. To a Chinese, it not only humiliated Dad but the whole household, servants included. This was not the only incident where Ah Kwan found American customs upsetting. One day Dad came home with some boxing gloves and encouraged the boys to learn to box with him. Filial piety (Confucian obligations to one's parents) said a son should NEVER hit his father.

Ah Kwan was horrified. Dad once even had Bob shoot him in the butt with a BB gun to see how strong it was—it raised a nasty red welt. Dad was sorry he had suggested it.

My interest in sports grew as I could now join teams in school. I was the best high jumper in my grade, using the old scissors kick, and became an avid field hockey player. The British army soldiers played field hockey for fitness and recreation and passed the sport on to their Indian recruits. The Indian men's field hockey team won the Olympics in 1948 and were the best in the world for many years. We tried to emulate them with an attacking game. When I came to America in 1951, I ran into trouble with coaches for continuing this style.

Although we were getting older and had fewer illnesses, we still had some medical problems. Mom took me to Macao, the Portuguese colony only a short amphibious plane ride from Hong Kong, for a visit. It was a gambling mecca and very different from Hong Kong. On the flight back I became sick. An appendectomy was necessary, and I spent an entire week in a hospital bed. The inactivity was debilitating. Even though I was athletic and in good physical condition when entering the hospital, I could barely stand up by myself one week later. The sole entertainment was the birth of a baby boy to my doctor's wife. The doctor had bright red hair and the tiny baby had a full head of hair even redder than his father's. It caused a sensation in the hospital where almost every baby had black hair.

The short flight to Macao, a Portuguese colony, was a popular vacation trip. In July 1948 we were on a picnic with some friends when something happened we didn't immediately understand. One of Bob's classmates at Central British School was with us on the picnic. She went home early because her parents were returning from a Cathay Pacific flight to Macao. The flight had not arrived.

The next day we learned their PBY Catalina flying boat, the same plane on which I had recently flown, had vanished. Fishermen brought in an unconscious survivor, but it took until the following afternoon before they found the plane wreckage. There were bullet holes in the fuselage and the pilot had been shot. It took a little while to decide who had jurisdiction over the incident; the British whose plane it was, the Portuguese in whose water it crashed, or the Chinese whose citizenship the survivor claimed.

After Portuguese interrogation, the survivor admitted he was part of a group of four hijackers who had taken over the plane. Several of the passengers were millionaires and carrying gold or cash. The plan was to land on a secluded island, rob the passengers and hold them for ransom. The survivor claimed one passenger protested and got into a scuffle with the hijackers. The pilot tried to help the passenger, and in the melee the pilot was shot and fell over the controls. The plane crashed killing all aboard except one hijacker who jumped out of an emergency exit just before the plane crashed. This was the first hijacking of a commercial airliner in the world. There were no specific laws against it and the jurisdiction was unclear. What to do? Evidently the hijacker remained in a Macao jail until 1951. One report said the Portuguese took him to the Chinese border, told him to run and shot him as an escapee. Another said his Chinese comrades shot him for naming his accomplices. Or the new Chinese Communist government had him killed in an *accident*. Regardless, problem solved! Both of our friend's parents had been on the plane. Mom briefly talked about adopting the orphaned children but, after a short period contacting relatives, they flew to Canada to live with their uncle.

There were two other plane crashes while we were in Hong Kong. In February 1949 a Cathay Pacific DC-3 crashed into the hillside near Braemar Reservoir following an aborted landing in the fog at Kai Tak. A long time after the incident I learned that Bruce and Bob had decided to explore the site. They took the Star Ferry across the bay to get near the scene where they found British soldiers with Bren guns guarding the area. The boys crept up to nearby bushes but decided it was too dangerous and pulled back. Later reports indicated the plane was carrying a load of gold bars for the Chinese nationalists. The boys told no one else of their adventure as I told no one about the cobra.

At the end of the next school year I was first in my class, received a one-year full scholarship—worth US$15—and skipped a grade. I tried to turn the scholarship down and give it to the next highest student, the Chinese girl, but the school would not let me. Imagine—an American and a Chinese were tops in their class in a British school!

The school was now admitting more non-British students so it decided to change its name to King George V School, now known as KGV, and honor a previous king of England. The governor of Hong Kong, Sir Alexander Grantham, was invited to a large school ceremony for the name change. After the governor's speech, our headmaster announced an extra day's vacation in the governor's honor. I thought the vacation pledge was great.

The captain of the sixth form football (American soccer) team led a cheer for the governor. But I was excited about the holiday. Sitting near the front as I was in the lowest grade in the school, in my little American accented voice I said, "Three cheers for the vacation." There was dead silence. I suddenly realized I had done something terribly wrong. A nudge from a friend urged me to continue. "Hip hip hurrah!, hip hip hurrah, hip hip hurrah!" And the whole audience responded. I feared I would be sent to the vice principal's office for punishment. For quite some time I took a long detour around his office to avoid him. They did not cane girls, but

I wasn't sure. About a year later my father met the governor at a Rotary luncheon and the governor asked him, "Are you the father of the little girl who loves holidays?"

As we grew older Mom and Dad continued to expose us to life as it is, not a fairy tale version. One of these experiences was to attend the Japanese war crime trials. These trials occurred between March 1946 and December 1948, but I only went once. What I remember was the British victim describing the steps they dragged him up to the torture room. His memory was so vivid I felt it was me being dragged up-he described every step. It was then I realized torture was not necessarily to gain information but often "for the pleasure of it" for the interrogator.

Chinese have been avid kite flyers for centuries and make many types. We used cheap kites made of bamboo and rice paper. We bought string coated with glass so we could use it in kite wars. We would fly a kite out over the city and wait for a challenger. When one appeared, we would try to cross strings with it. If we let our kite out quickly the friction between the strings and the glass coating on our string might cut the opponent's string. You won when his kite floated away. These kite wars were a lot of fun and inexpensive. Bruce was particularly good at them.

Mom and Bob took formal Cantonese lessons. Mom could not seem to handle the tones. They came more easily to me, I think because I was younger. I found it amusing as Mom used her head to make the tones rise and fall. Cantonese has nine tones whereas Mandarin has only four, so there was a lot of head bobbing.

I liked to bargain using my limited street Cantonese. I would ask the price in English, then listen to the sellers discuss what to ask this American. They had different markups for different groups such as tourists, Americans, British and so forth. The salesman would state the price and I would then reply *tai guai* (too expensive) in Cantonese and offer about half the price, or even less, again in Cantonese. The bargaining had begun, and it was a sport everyone except the tourists enjoyed.

Bruce and I took chess lessons and all three of us took typing lessons. Bruce and I competed in one chess tournament but, when I had to play him, I dropped out. Mom felt typing and shorthand were essential skills and they certainly were very useful when we became older.

Bob did not like Hong Kong. He had not wanted to leave Punahou and Hawaii. He had many friends there and felt he was establishing a new home. Now here he was in another strange environment having to build anew. In Punahou we were all learning together—teachers welcomed and encouraged questions and mutual discussions. In KGV Bruce found a Master making a mistake, and the teacher hit him on the back of the head for being "*cheeky*." Students were to listen and learn, not challenge or question.

Bob found the British colonial attitude self-superior, even to the Americans. He thought the Americans were superior to the British because we had won the war and treated the Chinese as people, not just servants. He got a summer job as a cub reporter with the South China Morning Post, the local newspaper, attending and reporting on trials. Soon he began a column called *Teen Age Topics*. He also interviewed British teenagers when they came home to Hong Kong during their summer holidays. I was very proud of him. The column was quite successful.

When Betty Betz, an American writer for teenagers, came to Hong Kong. He met her at the airport, arranged for her to appear at Tiger Balm Palace (a local amusement park) and reported the coming appearance in his column. The event was mobbed. There were arrests, and it was the end of Bob's job. The reporter who replaced him wrote an unfavorable column about Bob's role in the affair. Life was *unfair* to him. He was humiliated and said so. He was not being a *trooper*, but I was learning it was not always wrong to complain—how else could things be improved? The trick was knowing how to do it. Mom was so upset she drank too much that day. Bob wrote it was the only time he saw her drunk, but I know she drank to excess on other occasions when she was under a great deal of stress, as in Tucson when Bruce was sick.

Bob and Bruce reacted to the British swagger by becoming very patriotic Americans. At school Bruce read "The Midnight Ride of Paul Revere" just to annoy the Brits. The boys admired the fitness of the British army soldiers being trained in Kowloon, but the Americans were physically bigger. Even the American ships were bigger. At this point Bob thought about becoming a pilot in the US Navy.

Justice in Hong Kong was not color blind. Mom got a ticket for not having a license for our dog and she went down to the police station. She waited as the judge handled other cases. When it was her turn, he looked up, apologized and asked her to come into his chambers where he said she only had to send him the notice and he would have torn it up—which he promptly did. In Hong Kong harsh justice was for Chinese who were thought to only respect power, not white people.

Poverty was everywhere but, because one could not solve all of it, there was a tendency not to try unless it was on your doorstep. One Christmas Eve it literally was. There was a small entryway to our walled and barb-wired house. We found a young boy, about twelve, crouched there curled up in a ball to keep warm. Although Hong Kong was hot in the summer, it could be cold in the winter. Mom asked Ah Kwan to find out about him. The boy had been sold by his parents because the family needed the money to survive. He was then smuggled into Hong Kong in the bottom of a boat. When he saw a chance, he ran away, but he had nowhere to go.

We brought him inside, gave him something to eat, a warm blanket and a place where he could sleep. In the morning he was gone—he had climbed over our fence and stolen the blanket. We did not begrudge him the blanket.

At the bottom of Ho Man Tin Hill was Waterloo Road where there were a bunch of shacks which housed small businesses. We bought our kites there and other small purchases. One day we noticed the walls of one of the stores was constructed from the packing crates used to ship our goods to Hong Kong. Our name was stamped on the walls! They also had a small dog who looked just like ours which had recently disappeared. Somehow Mom was able to get Tai Guai back but he quickly became very ill, his back legs paralyzed. Bob had to take him out and shoot him. He didn't say much about it, but was obviously upset.

Only six months after we arrived in Hong Kong Mom became chairwoman of the women's welcoming committee of the American Club. There was no Parent Teachers Association at our school, so she started one to raise funds to buy the school a piano. She succeeded, but the principal made it very clear to the ladies they were to have no role in the school except to raise funds. She made friends extremely easily and inspired others to get involved.

Dad found his experiences as Kodak manager of China challenging and interesting. He was at the top of his business career. The office on the Bund in Shanghai prospered as did the Hong Kong branch, and he regularly commuted between the two cities. Gradually the situation changed as the Communists won battle after battle and moved southeast.

In March 1949 at the Shanghai airport he noticed the wounded soldiers being unloaded from planes had fresh blood on their bandages. It was clearly time for him to leave Shanghai permanently. Dad's aide, Mr. Pih, knew just who to pay off, and he secured passage for Dad out to Hong Kong.

Six weeks later Shanghai fell to the Communists. The office manager, Grandi, stayed behind to try to continue business, as did some businessmen from other American companies. Eventually most of them left but their companies paid a ransom disguised as unpaid taxes. Business did not stop completely, but it was substantially reduced.

Meanwhile, the population of Hong Kong grew rapidly, fueled as it was by refugees from north China. One of Kodak's customers in Canton, up the Pearl River in China proper, was doing exceptionally well and Dad arranged a visit. He found Mr. Wong was underselling his competition but still making money. It occurred to Dad he always bought his film in Hong Kong. Mr. Wong was a smuggler, avoiding the Nationalist tax by paying cash in duty free Hong Kong and smuggling the film into Canton.

There was a general fear the Communists would come right down the coast and capture Hong Kong, which was practically defenseless. Dad found his family in danger again. The United States government ordered all citizens to evacuate. Since Bob and Bruce were now both teenagers, our parents decided to enroll them in boarding schools in the States to prepare them for American colleges. Mom and I traveled with them with the hope of possibly returning to Hong Kong after one school year if it were safe.

Our parents purchased a book listing New England prep schools, and with the help of friends who were visiting and had some knowledge of the schools, they choose Choate for Bob and Mount Hermon for Bruce. Bob questioned the decision to send them to separate schools. We had no home except each other. Our parents felt the boys were so different in skills and temperament they belonged in different schools.

In June 1949 we embarked on the President Polk for a sea voyage through the Suez Canal to New York City. Dad stayed in Hong Kong, alone again. His business future was uncertain, and he would again have to face it without his family. The fate of Hong Kong itself was unknown as it lay in the path of the Communist advance. I was sorry to leave Hong Kong because of all its vitality and challenges, but I don't think Bob was. He had not enjoyed living in a British colony. Both boys knew they would soon be separated from their family in boarding schools.

# VIII

This trip was our second refugee experience but much different from the first. A refugee is defined as "a person who has been forced to leave their country or home in order to escape war, persecution or natural disaster." We were war refugees, but not in desperate circumstances as we had been following the Pearl Harbor attack. We fled the Chinese Communists on an American ocean liner, the President Polk, taking a comfortable trip half-way around the world. The ship was four hundred and ninety-two feet long with room for ninety-six passengers and substantial cargo. It even had a swimming pool.

First we stopped in Manila where we could still see the superstructures of ships sunk in the Battle of Manila. Some reconstruction of the many destroyed buildings had been done, but the city remained a shadow of its former self. We found even familiar landmarks hard to locate as so much of the city still lay in ruins. It was not the world our parents or Bob remembered. Dad had taken a picture of what remained of our home when he visited right after the war. The picture showed our concrete steps in the middle of a field with no signs of a house. Now those same steps were still there but attached to a shack where people were living.

Bob was disappointed he did not see Felisa, nor did we see the Nashes who were now in Chicago. They had been in Manila when the Japanese invaded and spent the war in Santo Tomas prison camp and Los Banos. We were very grateful Dad had requested the transfer to Hawaii. Grace

117

Nash wrote in her memoir, *That We Might Live*[*], that she had been very concerned about a possible invasion and considered returning to America. Her husband said fine, but he was not going. He was successful in Manila and wanted to stay in his current job. She refused to leave without him. So… she stayed with their two small sons. In prison camp she sorely regretted her decision.

Years later people asked me about Pearl Harbor and our escape on the convoy and I always described how lucky we were. We could easily have been with the Nashes in Santo Tomas. Thanks to Dad acting on his concerns, we escaped being prisoners of war and almost starving to death. Here in Manila we were refugees again—this time fleeing the Chinese Communists—and Dad was getting us out in time again while he remained in Hong Kong.

On this two-month trip by ship Mom made a point of working on our secretarial skills. We knew some Pitman shorthand, the English system, and could type fairly well, although my hands remained so small I had to lift the left hand to hit the B key. In the mornings on board ship Mom would dictate a letter. We then each transcribed and typed the letter. It was mildly competitive for us and a very useful skill.

When computers became necessary, we did not have to learn to keyboard as we were already good typists. When I moved permanently to America Mom insisted I learn another shorthand system, Gregg. In college I took my notes mainly in Gregg, writing out key names or words in longhand. If someone asked to borrow my notes because they skipped class, I could easily say "yes," even though I resented the request—why should I attend classes and they benefit? One glance at my notes and they changed their minds.

We took side trips from the ship when Mom thought it would expand our education. In Penang we drove to a nature

---

[*] Nash, Grace. *That We Might Live*. Scottsdale, AZ. 1984

118

preserve where monkeys overwhelmed her to steal her bananas. We took a train up to Kuala Lumpur where we watched a fight between a cobra and a mongoose—the mongoose won. When loading the ship, workers dropped a case of mercury. Some of the containers shattered and mercury poured all over the deck. We gathered up a bottle of it and rubbed it on our silver coins, making them glitter—for a short while, until they turned grey. We did not know mercury was poisonous or its value.

While crossing the Bay of Bengal, we ran into a ferocious storm. Although the President Polk was a large ship, the waves were larger. The ship would rise to the crest of one wave, shudder, cascade down the other side, and submarine into the next swell. The crests were so high they covered the bow of the ship until we pulled up unto the next one. Mom was seasick below deck, but the three of us found a spot just under the bridge where we could watch the action without being washed away. It was thrilling and, to me, scary. After a while Bob and I went below deck.

Bruce, always curious and adventurous, wandered onto the lifeboat deck to see what was happening there. As he did so a huge surge of seawater knocked him off his feet and carried him along the deck. Then the ship rose to the next crest and the water rapidly retreated from the deck, again carrying him with it. There were no guardrails on the lifeboat deck in order to facilitate launching the boats and he quickly realized he could be swept overboard. He grabbed a tie rope as he was propelled under a lifeboat and frantically held on as the water rushed past him. As soon as he could he jumped up and ran back into the covered area of the boat. He knew he had been foolish and did not tell Mom. It was another brush with death for Bruce.

We traveled on to Colombo, then Bombay (Mumbai) where the poverty appeared to be much worse than in Hong

Kong. Parents maimed their children so their unfortunate offspring could be successful beggars. Mom could hardly believe a parent would do that to her child, but extreme poverty could make people do unimaginable acts. She also took us to an Indian cremation site to introduce us to their burial practices. Although India was now independent, the vestiges of colonialism and class were strong. A banker friend took her to The Club where men in trade, i.e. businessman who were not bankers, lawyers or doctors, were excluded. Children born to British parents in India were known as Nationals, not Subjects, so those who could afford to do so sent their pregnant wives *home* to England for their birthing.

After Bombay it was on to Karachi, Pakistan, and up the Red Sea towards Suez where we disembarked to take the train to Cairo. Jews were strongly advised to stay on the ship because of strong anti-Jewish sentiment in Egypt following the Arab-Israeli war the preceding year. We visited the pyramids, rode camels, and bought small scarabs (I still have one). Riding a camel is different from riding a horse, particularly when it gets up and down. To rise, they first extend their front knees, pushing you backwards, then they straighten their back legs pitching you forward, then they straighten the front legs again, leveling off. When you pull back on the reins to slow down, the camel's head can end up in your lap, but the camel sometimes keeps going.

Our guide, Ali Baba, scared Mom when he cornered her alone in Cheop's pyramid and insisted she give him her purse, which she did. He took her cash and handed the purse back. She said he was worse than the forty thieves because he then had the nerve to expect her to hire him again the next day.

On our way back to Cairo we were stopped in traffic and threatened by a mob who called us dirty Jews. Bob said it was as scary as Pearl Harbor because it was physically in our faces and Dad was not there. I think he thought it was his responsibility to protect the family, and he did not feel up to the task. Egypt was a harrowing experience for Mom too as she tried to expose her children to important world cultures while protecting them from harm. She must have sorely missed the support of her husband. Her occasional bouts of crying probably reflected this, but she didn't complain. She tried to be a trooper, but she was not totally successful. We visited the National Museum in Cairo and saw the amazing treasures of Tutankhamen but were relieved to return to the safety of the ship in Port Said.

At sea again, we stopped at Naples, Pompeii, Rome, Civitavecchia, Genoa and Marseille before sailing across the Atlantic to New York City. We saw a lot of fascinating things but in the back of all our minds were thoughts of Dad marooned in Hong Kong, vulnerable to a Communist takeover, and ourselves with the unknown ahead. Crossing the Atlantic, Bob became very apprehensive about life in another new school. He thought mainly in negatives—he was not a good athlete; he was not smart; his eyesight was not good. He became physically sick with poor digestion and possibly worms. We had the worm cure several times in Hong Kong, but perhaps he still harbored some. He became depressed. Bruce, as usual, buried himself in military and adventure books. My future was unknown but simple. I was to tag along with Mom wherever she went. I had the fewest worries.

We disembarked from the President Polk and proceeded to the Roosevelt Hotel in New York City. Our room had a black and white television set—this was the first one we had ever seen. We picked up a new Ford car at a factory across the Hudson River in New Jersey and headed towards Connecticut. Mom had never driven around a clover leaf. In our new car she ended up driving around more than one circle. So she stopped and asked a policeman how to get back across the Hudson. He gave her directions and off we went again—only to return shortly in front of the same policeman. This new world was certainly confusing.

The drive up through the Connecticut River valley to the prep schools was spectacular. There were tobacco farms with their distinctive barns with alternately tilted slat siding to allow air circulation to dry the leaves. There were old stone fences surrounding fields which became overgrown when they were abandoned. The landscape was unfamiliar to us. The schools themselves were physically impressive, but both my brothers were understandably nervous. The decision to send them to separate schools meant they would be isolated from each other's immediate support. They would be as alone as I had been in Oakland, California, staying with the Pyes, although they were older.

The schools enrolled the boys a week early due to our special circumstances and Mom and I drove on to Rochester. We stopped in Mendon to visit the small farm our parents purchased when we were in Manila. Mom weighed building a cabin there so we would have a home base in the future. Then it was back to New England to go to Wellesley, Massachusetts, where Mom found a job as a housemother at Tenacre, a private girls school.

## On October 1, 1949, Communists proclaimed victory in China

In his autobiography, *Story Time*[*], Bob described Choate as difficult at first (when had a new school not been difficult) but there were sympathetic teachers and he grew to appreciate Choate. I noticed when he had trouble with a particular teacher or subject he would comment the teacher did not like him. He was always ready to dispute with anyone if they

[*] Gordon, Robert M. Jr. *Story Time*. 2011

122

did not agree with him. Both boys were very patriotic and thinking of joining the navy or air force after school and they were quick to defend the United States when they sensed it was being attacked, verbally or physically. I thought Bob was slow to listen to other people's opinions before countering them with his own. He seldom simply ignored a position he thought wrong.

Choate, with Mom's approval, held Bob back a year to give him time to adjust to his new circumstances. His intestinal problems returned and he was sent to a hospital in New Haven for tests. They thought he might have malaria or dysentery left over from Hong Kong. He improved and soon returned to Choate. By Christmastime his health and his academics were much better.

Bruce faced many of the same problems Bob did, but his school was quite different. At Mount Hermon manual labor by all the boys was required for ten hours per week. Since he arrived before the fall term started, Bruce worked on the school farm until classes began. He enjoyed the outdoor labor. When school opened he joined the other boys in doing many menial chores such as waiting tables, digging ditches and cleaning bathrooms. He continued to read many adventure books which helped to ease his sense of isolation. He was an average student but adapted well to his new environment and learned to be proud of a job well done, no matter how humble it was.

Mom's job as a housemother at Tenacre gave us both room and board and paid for my tuition in the school. This was a difficult period for me and I was homesick for what seemed a long time. Most nights I cried myself to sleep. How could I be so homesick when my mother was literally across the street? I knew I had to be a trooper and not complain.

The Communist conquest of China was not my parents' fault. I had little contact with my mother, almost no contact with my brothers until Christmas, and none with my father. When people are depressed, they are more susceptible to illness, and I caught what was probably the flu. The school nurse, Mrs. Dunbar, was known for prescribing enemas for every illness (the Dunbar Special), so the girls did not go to her unless it was absolutely necessary. By the time I visited the nurse, I had a raging fever and was put in the infirmary for a week. Eventually I became accustomed to the school but was never happy there.

Mom never ceased her efforts to make me clothes-conscious. Boston was very cold in the winter, so she bought me two coats, one a warm brown one and the other a lighter black jacket, both with matching hats. Every Sunday my class marched together along the main street to church, dressed appropriately. One Sunday I left my brown hat in a locker in a building closed on Sundays, so I wore my black hat with the brown coat to church. Mom happened to see me walking by her dorm with my class and noticed the hat. To make the point that all outfits must be coordinated, she took away my warm coat for a time. It certainly impressed me but primarily that clothes were important to her, not to me. She was trying hard to make me into the kind of girl she thought would be successful, i.e. find a wealthy husband, but I was not listening. I don't think it was money she felt would make me happy but the freedom from worries she imagined wealth brought.

At Tenacre I took tennis lessons with another girl. I learned later her father wanted her to learn to play and paid for both of us to take lessons. When she got frustrated and gave up, the lessons ceased, but I had found a new sport I enjoyed.

At Christmastime the four of us spent the holiday together in a small rented house on the Tenacre property. We tried ice skating and saw snow falling for the first time. We took a short tour of Boston's historical sites. Bob, Bruce and I discussed our loneliness and our possible futures. We were closer than many siblings because we shared each other's history and no one else's. To give us something of a home base for the first time in our lives, Mom went ahead with the idea of a small cabin in Mendon. She arranged for its construction on the plot of land we had looked at earlier in the fall. The plan pleased Bob as we would now have a home base although it wouldn't feel like a real home until we lived there.

In 1949 Dad sold our house on Ho Man Tin Hill as he was unsure we would return. The price was good but the value of the Hong Kong dollar fell rapidly against the American dollar as people desperately fled China. Conversion into American dollars caused a considerable loss. He moved into the Hong Kong Club. Although the Communists did not attempt to capture Hong Kong, they located goods through Eastern European countries, and business in Shanghai declined. Grandi, his manager in Shanghai, decided to leave. The Communists demanded US $50,000 for his freedom but he managed to depart without ransom because he was not an American citizen.

One day, in Hong Kong, Mr. Wong, the smuggler, appeared in Dad's office. He was distraught. From Dad's book *Something Worthwhile*:

> *"Me smuggler. Now no can smuggle. No can make honest living. No can live."*
>
> *Wong moaned and swayed in his chair as he went on.*
>
> *"No good daughter tell police I smuggle, put gold in hiding place. Police come, pound on door. Go out back door, hide. Now come Hong Kong." He paused to look me in the face.*
>
> *"Police got gold. Daughter get picture in the paper, medal. Me old man. No money, no wife, no children. No can get job. No can live..." His voice trailed off.*

In the spring, business picked up in Hong Kong as residents and tourists lost their fear of Communist invasion. In June Dad flew back to the United States, joined mother and me in Boston and we continued on to Rochester so he could report to his office.

When school let out for the summer, the boys joined us in the partially completed Mendon cabin. They helped dig a hole for an outhouse, went hunting and enjoyed the outdoors. Mom and I set to work sewing curtains and setting up housekeeping. It was primitive living, but we were glad to be together. The biggest problem turned out to be water for the cabin. Dad hired a local dowser who came with a divining rod and recommended we dig in one spot. I tried the rod myself and sensed it pull down. Dad hired a driller to come in and he dug a long way without hitting enough water. He kept saying a gusher was just a little further down but when Dad offered him double or nothing if he struck enough water, the contractor didn't take the deal.

Dad and his friend Max Dunn moved further down the hill to an area with lots of green plants growing and dug an open well by hand. Soon they found water but kept digging to find more. They used a pump to keep water from accumulating as they dug. It was dangerous work due to the possibility of the sides collapsing or of poisoning from the pump's fumes settling in the bottom where they were digging. Eventually they found enough water, installed a pump, and we had running water in the cabin. We all have fond memories of this short period as we were working together to build a home.

**On June 25th, 1950, North Korea invaded South Korea**

Bob registered for the draft in Meriden, Connecticut, a small town near Choate, but he was still in school so could not be drafted. He started having dates with girls in the vicinity and struggled with his new feelings. He had strong moral values, as did our father, and was shocked by what he believed were other people's immoral activities. Being a teenager was hard enough, but he felt like a foreigner as well.

At the end of the summer Dad, Mom and I headed back to Hong Kong via Europe. The Korean War appeared remote and Dad was eager to return to work. He thought it might be possible to continue to work with the Chinese Communists. We stopped in Scotland where we attended the Braemar Games in pouring rain, then on to Switzerland where a cold Mom developed at the Games turned into pneumonia. We stopped in Switzerland for several days as she recovered. I spent the time sitting in the village square in front of our hotel learning how to knit in the European style from the old ladies relaxing there. They only spoke French, so I was glad I had studied French in the British schools. Then on to Delhi, India, where we planned to go to the Taj Mahal.

Traffic in Delhi was heavy, and we arrived at the railroad station just as the train for Agra was pulling out of the station.

"But you may be able to still catch the train," someone said.

"How?"

"It stops in New Delhi before it finally leaves for Agra. Perhaps you can beat it there."

Dad didn't hesitate.

"I will double your fare if you can beat the train to New Delhi," Dad said to the nearest taxi driver.

We jumped in and, as our taxi pulled out of the train station, another man jumped in the front passenger seat and grabbed the horn. People, pedicabs, cows and peddlers jammed the streets. One man blew the horn almost continuously, and the other drove like a mad man.

We made it! We caught the train in New Delhi and continued on to Agra.

There we saw the Taj Mahal by moonlight. The sight was so mesmerizing that, many years later when I returned to the Taj, I asked a friend to photograph me sitting there on a bench, remembering the experience with my parents. In those days few Indians visited the Taj and there was only a smattering of Western tourists. It was eerily quiet and peaceful under a full moon. Dad was feeling more positive about business in China as it now appeared the Communists would continue to trade with American companies, so we traveled on to Hong Kong.

When we returned in the summer of 1950, we rented an apartment on MacDonnell Road, the second stop up on the Peak Tram. Promptly Ah Kwan showed up at our door and asked for his job back. He had worked a short time for an English family, but was fired. He did not cook in the manner they preferred and confused jam, jelly and jello because he used American terms. I also suspect he was not subservient enough for their taste. We were happy to have him back.

I returned to KGV in much more difficult circumstances. First, to get to school I took the Peak Tram down the mountain, a rickshaw across to the Star Ferry birth, the ferry across the bay to Kowloon, and a bus to the bottom of the hill near the school. From there it was only a short walk up to KGV. I took the reverse trip home. At that time, no tunnel or bridge existed between Kowloon and Hong Kong Island so driving was impossible. It was a long trip to and from school for a twelve-year-old.

The academic challenge was even more difficult. I had skipped a full grade just before I left the year before, so I was now two years ahead of my age. I had missed beginning Latin, a year of French and even found other subjects, which seemed the same, were different in an English school. KGV stressed geography, and it is an important subject, but it was almost ignored during my nine months at Tenacre. It was a struggle to catch up, but I loved Hong Kong and was comfortable academically after a month or so. Hong Kong was so exciting!

One evening Dad, Mom and I visited the apartment of some of my parents' friends. We rang the bell and, as we were entering the vestibule, their dog (a German Shepherd) walked up and bit me. I didn't even get beyond the entryway. Rabies was common in Hong Kong so shots were routinely given unless it was shown the dog was not rabid. In this case, we had the dog, so I suffered through painful rabies shots for one week while they quarantined the dog. He did not have rabies, so the shots ceased.

One day Mom received a telephone call from Dad.

"Did you give our houseboy (not Ah Kwan) a check for $10,000 to take to the bank?"

"No, of course not."

"He is at the bank trying to cash your check. Please examine your checkbook and see if any checks are missing."

She did and found several missing.

The police at the bank arrested the houseboy who said he had been approached by someone who knew he worked at our apartment and regularly took his paycheck to the bank to cash. The friend asked him to take checks out of Mom's checkbook and give them to the forger which he did. The forger practiced Mom's signature on the checks, then gave the best one back to the houseboy to take to the bank.

The bank teller, on looking at the check, noticed it was for a much larger amount than the houseboy usually received, so he reported it to his superiors. The bank officers called Dad and Dad called Mom. No, of course she had not written the check. The police arrested the houseboy but his accomplice, who had been waiting outside the bank for him to come out with the cash, had fled. The houseboy was tried, convicted and served one month in jail. The judge also sentenced him to ten strokes of the lash just before release. The whipping was done to prevent people from committing a crime just to go to jail where they received free food and lodging. The prison cells faced towards the whipping post so the prisoners could watch others being flogged before it was their turn. The most-guilty party, the actual forger, was never apprehended.

At first the Korean War went well for the North Koreans as the South Koreans and United Nations forces barely held on to the Pusan Perimeter. In September 1950 MacArthur's troops successfully invaded Inchon and pushed the North Korean forces back. By October US forces had crossed the 38th parallel and moved on to occupy Pyongyang, the North Korean capital. Soon Allied forces approached the Chinese border. To assess the situation President Truman sent Ambassador-at-large Philip Jessup to China. As President of the American Club in Hong Kong, Dad was invited to meet with him at the American Consulate. They spoke privately and Dad emphasized the danger of American participation in a ground war in China. He never knew if his opinions reached Truman but the President refused to let MacArthur invade China.

## On November 4th, 1950, the Chinese Communists invaded North Korea

American troops were caught by a surprise massive Chinese invasion across the Yalu River into North Korea, and reeled back towards the south. On December 15th the US declared a state of emergency.

At the same time the UN forces were retreating from North Korea, we were celebrating Christmas in Hong Kong. Mom invited some American sailors to join us, a tradition we had followed for years. While they were at our apartment overlooking the harbor, they received a telephone call from their ship—they were ordered to return immediately. An hour later we saw their vessel, the USS Albuquerque, pull out of the harbor. The situation must be serious for the navy to make such a rapid change in plans. I received two new suitcases as Christmas presents that year, so it was clear Dad again would get his family out of harm's way as soon as he could.

Meanwhile in the United States Bob and Bruce needed a place to spend their holidays. At least the year before Mom and I were near enough so she could secure a house for Christmas vacation. This winter the boys stayed with Max and Grace Dunn in Mendon. Max took them pheasant hunting with their English setter dogs. Bruce shot a bird on the wing and Max was duly impressed. They enjoyed going hunting on the farm with Max and his sons.

On January 1st, 1951, the American Consul-General in Hong Kong announced all non-essential US citizens should leave. Mom and I packed our bags and Dad moved back into the Hong Kong Club. We flew to Japan, refugees for the third time. Communist China was an ally of North Korea and there was a possibility the war in North Korea would spread into a general war with China—in fact, General MacArthur advocated such a strategy, though opposed by President Truman. In essence, we were already at war with China as US troops, under the UN banner, were fighting Chinese soldiers. Technically, the Chinese government called their soldiers *volunteers* so there was no declaration of war by China.

On January 7th I woke up in a Japanese artist's house opposite Mount Fuji. There had been a fresh snowfall and Mount Fuji looked like a birthday cake with white frosting. In the afternoon we caught a flight to Honolulu but stopped at Midway Island on January 8th for repairs. We finally arrived in Honolulu on January 7th, having crossed the International Dateline. Two thirteenth birthdays in one year!

Mom later said she originally planned to go back to Tenacre in Wellesley but I persuaded her to go to Honolulu instead because I loved Punahou and she would be closer to Dad. I was learning to speak up for what I wanted rather than always being a trooper and never complaining. We took an apartment in the Manoa valley and I re-enrolled in Punahou. Dad's book *Milly* is sometimes incorrect on what grades I was in—the changes confused everyone except Mom.

Although Punahou said I did not test well enough to keep up academically in the grade I was in when I left Punahou several years earlier, Mom insisted I return to my friends' class—now the eighth grade. I was happy to give up the extra grade I skipped in Hong Kong but did not want to go back two grades and miss the few friends I knew. I struggled with some issues others did not have. I used words from several languages without knowing they were not English. I struggled with tenses until I learned the past perfect, the pluperfect and the plus que parfait were the same tense in different languages—American, English and French. Every school felt it was stronger academically than my previous school. Soon I was doing well in the eighth grade with my old friends.

My principal teacher was Mr. Greenwell. He maintained we should go to school to learn, not to put in time, so we tackled units together as a class. At the end of a unit we would all take a test. The goal was to have everyone get over a certain grade. After the test, all those who did well turned around and tutored those who did not until everyone succeeded. To my surprise, those of us doing the tutoring learned the material far better than we would have if we only learned it for ourselves. Then we would all pile into cars and go on an expedition to the pineapple fields or swimming and enjoy the reward for a job well done. Years later I heard he was directed to stop this practice because some parents complained we were not always in class. I hope this is not true as he was the best teacher I ever had.

This time at Punahou I enjoyed my first date. Every year the school has a big fair called the Carnival. In my class was a Japanese-American boy, Asa Akinaka, and we went to the Carnival together. In Hawaii, Japanese-American families objected more strongly to cross dating than haoli (Caucasian) families did—my mother certainly made no objection. In the eighth-grade dating simply meant we strolled around the fair together.

In April General MacArthur was relieved of his command in spite of loud protests in America. Ambassador Jessup later became a major target of Senator McCarthy, accused of Communist sympathies. Dad's business position in Hong Kong deteriorated again. On May 18, 1951, America put an embargo on any trade with China. Dad had hoped to continue to do business with the Communists through Hong Kong, and so had his dealers, but the new regulations prohibited it. He called a meeting to explain the new situation to them. Dad wrote:

> *When I asked for questions, up jumped a young man whom I had never seen before, and it was soon obvious that he was a Communist anxious to do battle with Uncle Sam. He saw the embargo as a capitalist declaration of war on China. By the embargo the United States was seeking to undermine the livelihood of the people of China, and the Eastman Kodak Company, by complying with the embargo, was shamelessly attacking the very people listening to him. Speaking alternately in Cantonese and broken English, the young man then turned his fire on me personally. It was presumptuous of me to schedule a meeting of photo dealers without the prior approval of the newly formed socialist union of photo workers. It was I who was masterminding the impoverishment of the photo workers of China. It was I and my stooges who sold our goods at exorbitant prices to defraud*

*the people of China of the capital it needed to build*
*its economy. We were not needed, and China would*
*prove to the world that the American embargo was*
*another paper tiger.*

*Emotionally he concluded, "You!" He pointed his fin-*
*ger at me.*

*"You! You take the profit from China. You rob*
*Chinese people. You no good for China."*

*He paused to catch his breath, and I heard a murmur*
*of disapproval quickly hushed as he went on.*

*"You! You running dog of Wall Street! You go home!"*

Dad's office evacuated all its American employees, and the staff was reduced to eight people. Although he could have remained to manage the Hong Kong office with limited business, Dad felt marginalized and asked for a transfer back to the US. He was not fully aware of the strength of McCarthyism on the mainland and the suspicion of anyone with ties to Communist China. He wrote about this decision:

*I felt I knew China, the Chinese and how to do*
*business with the new regime. I thought this ability*
*would be valued, but the anti-Communist feeling in*
*America was so strong that perhaps I was more sus-*
*pect than valued.*

# IX

It did not work out well for my father and I wondered later if he regretted leaving Hong Kong. He was only forty-seven years old and his career was side-tracked through no fault of his own.

In June Dad picked up Mom and me in Honolulu and we returned to Rochester. After checking in with Dad's office, we moved to a hotel in New York City. Mom started looking for a house in the suburbs so Dad could commute to his new job in the city. They bought a house in New Rochelle from which Dad could take a train to Manhattan.

The cutoff birthdate for the local school, Albert Leonard Junior High, was January 1st, which Mom discovered before going to enroll me. I had dropped one grade going back to Punahou, and she did not think I needed to drop another grade. She told the school my birthdate was December 7th, 1937, placing me in ninth grade. I had no problem with bending the rules, as in this case, although Bob found such actions disturbing. The administration expressed concern I would have trouble keeping up with the class due to my performance on their tests, but with the December birthdate, I qualified. Years later educators realized how tests were culturally biased. I always understood. It took eight years before I could revert to my actual birthdate on all my official documents.

The next few months were some of the worst of my life. I was even more of a misfit in Albert Leonard Junior High than I had been in my other schools, and a good bit of it was my own fault. Academically I was way ahead of most of my classmates (although the tests I had taken did not show this). I had studied French, Latin, English literature, history and comprehensive geography and knew a little Cantonese and Spanish. I didn't know anything about what really mattered—like the Brooklyn Dodgers and clothes.

In some ways I thought I was superior to my classmates. I had few social skills and yet, more than anything else, I wanted to have friends. I was physically underdeveloped, short and still a year young for my class. Dad complained about my rapid mood swings and general hyperactivity. I would come home after school and cry every afternoon. Then I saw a white Persian kitten in the window of a store and I just had to have her. She was a purebred and Mom said we couldn't afford her. I wrote to my brother Bruce, who was always frugal and might have some money.

"Dear Bruce," I wrote. "I have found a beautiful white Persian kitten I would like to buy. She costs $35. Mom says they don't have the money for her. Would you be willing to lend me the money? When she grows up, I will breed her and sell the kittens and pay you back."

His response was immediate and clear. "No. It is not a good investment. Too much can happen."

I was crest fallen. Not much later I received another letter from Bruce. "I still think it is a bad investment but here is a check for the $35."

Mom had written him and told him how lonely I was and he then sent the $35 as a gift. The kitten saved my sanity. She always knew how unhappy I was and let me cry into her silky white fur at will. Today we would call her a pet therapist.

Kitsue and I discussed my problems. I needed to figure out how to make friends. Perhaps the key was to like the things they liked. I read the sports pages so I could talk to the boys and made wardrobe changes to match the clothes the girls were wearing. I tried not to talk about myself or my background. I was not selling out—I was adapting. Every time I changed schools there was an awful moment when everyone turned and starred at the new girl. Tootsie rolls and bubble gum wouldn't work anymore.

A new musical opened on Broadway in March 1951, *The King and I.* The heroine and her young son are on a ship arriving in Thailand and he worries about being new and different. She sings a song with him: *I Whistle a Happy Tune, and No One Ever Knows I'm Afraid.* I started humming this tune silently to myself when I was nervous, and it helped me over many difficult moments.

In 1953 I moved on to the 10th grade at New Rochelle High School. By this time, I was adjusting both academically and athletically. I tried out for the field hockey team and shocked the coach. I played an aggressive game as we had in Hong Kong.

I attacked opponents as they were hitting the ball and tried to steal it. Whistle.

Coach: "You can't do that. You might get hit."

Me: "I do."

I hit the ball in the air. Whistle.

Coach: "You can't do that. You might hit someone else with the ball."

Me: "It happens."

I flicked the ball into the air. Whistle.

Coach: again. "You might hurt someone."

Oh well, I wanted to play, so I concentrated on what one needed to do to play American field hockey. I was a trooper and didn't argue with the coach. Perhaps I should have. Many years later I watched the finals of the women's field hockey Olympics in Atlanta, Georgia—the women were playing the aggressive game I had played when I first came to New Rochelle, but with new protective gear. By adapting my play to the game they were playing in New Rochelle, I competed on varsity teams in high school and college. Perhaps I would have been a better player if I had continued the more aggressive game we played in Hong Kong. Maybe being a trooper was not always the best strategy.

The high school had an athletic field with tennis courts near our house and during the summer I walked over there to hit tennis balls with the young college student who supervised the courts. She had competed in the New York State Junior tennis championships, so she was an accomplished player. I enjoyed rallying with her, but we did not play matches because she was much better than I was. She was attending Mount Holyoke, so I thought I might like to go there too.

In the spring of my sophomore year I was tapped to join a sorority. I knew I was doing better socially but couldn't fathom the popular girls wanted me in their club. I expressed my surprise to my best friend, Barbara Hang.

"I can't believe they would ask me to join. Did you get rushed?"

"Of course not," she said. "I am half Jewish."

"Why does that matter?" I asked. I was still suffering from the racial and ethnic blinders I had in China—I simply did not notice these differences.

"Look around," she said.

And then I noticed all the sorority girls were white Protestants in a school with many blacks, Italians, Jews and Catholics.

The prejudice shocked me and I at once resigned from the sorority. My resignation particularly galled the sorority girls. They were not used to rejection. The new recruits had chosen me as chairman of the pledges' party where we celebrate the new class. They would have to find someone else.

Of course, now I was shunned by all the popular girls. So much for learning to adapt. I should have stayed in the sorority and tried to change things. I needed to learn when NOT to be a trooper. Sometimes one needs to be a force for change and not simply have a stiff upper lip or never complain. My social life became worse again, although it was better than the ninth grade. Our tenth grade was grouped academically and my classmates, the highest group, was predominately Jewish. They did not shun me. However, Mom decided I needed to get away from this situation so she determined to send me to Dana Hall in Wellesley, Massachusetts, as a boarding student. Sending me to Dana put even more financial pressure on my parents but permitted me to escape from my problems at New Rochelle High School.

I had begun to mature physically and grow taller although I did not reach five foot five until I was in college. The summer before I went away to Dana, Mom signed me up for lessons to improve my appearance. She wanted me to attract boys and eventually the right husband. So I attended a short course in modeling at the John Robert Powers School of Modeling in New York. I took the train by myself in to their studio in the city and learned how to stand and sit and wear make-up. It would have been great for Mom but I wasn't interested. Why do we sometimes push our children into things we want?

About this time, Mom went shopping in New York and stopped at Bergdorf Goodman, a very exclusive store. She bought an outfit for herself which was on sale. She rarely bought anything for herself at this time of financial pressure but she couldn't resist this outfit and the price was right. She purchased a lovely champagne colored silk suit. While coming back on the train, she lost a loose fabric covered button. She came home in tears. She had finally bought what she really desired, and it was defective! Never in my life did I cry over clothes or even dream about them.

Dad's adjustment to life commuting to work in Manhattan was at least as difficult as mine was in school. In 1952 he made a quick business trip back to Hong Kong. While there he invited an old friend, a retired Air Force colonel, to dinner. The friend had been born in India, spoke Hindustani and Cantonese, had graduated from Yale, and in WWII had bossed the construction of landing fields in China. After dinner they played billiards. He asked Dad how business was in New York. From Dad's book, *Something Worthwhile*:

> *"Alright," I answered, and then added, "but I find it confusing after Hong Kong. I don't think I've gotten into the swing of it yet."*
>
> *"That's all I wanted to know," he interrupted me, and summed it up, "I don't think I could make a living there any more than I can here."*
>
> *Two mornings later the newspapers reported he had hung himself from the chandelier in his room at the Hong Kong Hotel.*

New York was a struggle for Dad, and his friend's suicide touched him deeply. Dad commented that he saw beggars and millionaires and he didn't fit in with either. His job in wholesale distribution was routine and unchallenging and the daily commute was exhausting, In Honolulu and China he had been the boss, but now he was just another employee. He needed to keep his job for the sake of his family. In those years Kodak had a reputation as being quite paternalistic and it tried to keep good employees. Nowadays when businesses downsize, employees are fired. His job in China had disappeared but at least he had a job in New York. He expected his experiences in China would be appreciated in the United States but instead it seemed to be a burden. In the era of McCarthyism, the Communist conquest of China had tainted his business career. While I felt Kodak had stood by Dad, Bob felt they had abandoned him. Dad was no longer on the fast track to business success.

Mom took a part-time job as a florist for additional income and to fill the time with the boys and me away at school. Mom's having a job insulted Dad—he felt it showed he was not a good provider. When she had to work extra hours for the Christmas rush, he insisted she resign. They had both been taught a man's job was to provide for his family and a woman's job was finding a husband and caring for him, their home and children. Bob felt Mom had undermined Dad's self-respect. I felt Dad had not understood how important it was for her to be doing something productive. Bruce said this was the only time he heard either of them mention the possibility of divorce.

Mom became increasingly weak and listless and eventually, on her doctor's recommendation, she had a hysterectomy. Her headaches became worse, not better. To keep busy, she joined a Shakespeare study group and took flower arranging classes. She redecorated our new house, putting in a picture window overlooking the lake, and repainting and wallpapering everything she could. She even began making some of our clothes, which I did not always appreciate.

This was the same woman who, when single, had worked her way around the world by herself! Mom and Dad were suffering economically and emotionally from our moves, but they had made a commitment to each other. I felt her headaches were partially the result of these problems as was their relationship with each other. Should Dad have looked for another job? Should Mom have insisted more strongly that she needed an outside job for her own fulfillment?

My brothers had summer jobs, and I wanted one too so I could buy a portable typewriter. While walking down the street in New Rochelle I saw a sign in the window of the five and ten cent store: *Help Wanted*. I needed to prove myself by finding a job without any help from my parents. Somehow, I found the nerve to walk in and apply for a summer job.

They gave me a math test. There was one question I could not answer because one needed to know the number of bushels in a peck, and I did not. The examiner corrected my paper and found one answer blank.

"Oh," I said. "That is because I don't know how many bushels are in a peck."

"One bushel equals four pecks," she responded.

"All right," I said. "Then the answer to the question would be twenty."

"Correct," she replied. "Then you got them all right."

"No, I didn't," I contested. "I didn't know that when I took the test."

She said nothing but hired me.

My failure to do well on entry tests to new schools made me aware of how biased tests are to the norms in their areas. Gaping holes persisted in our education as we bounced from one school to another. I never learned the seven times table and forever switched the numbers to multiply eight times seven and not seven times eight. In the tropics we could not answer winter questions not because we weren't smart but because we had no experience with snow or ice. I did poorly on English math tests because I didn't know their currency and measurements. We used words from different languages (Hawaiian, Tagalog, Pidgin, Cantonese, Spanish, French etc.) without knowing they were not English. Sometimes we used English spelling and sometimes American spelling. I even had trouble with table manners-being ambidextrous I frequently switched my fork from my right to my left hand, or vice versa. I felt very comfortable with English table manners.

Meanwhile Bruce and Bob were finishing at their prep schools. All the boys at Mount Hermon had to work ten hours per week maintaining the school. The school had its own cows and dairy. Bruce worked in the fields for a while and then was assigned to the creamery. His job there was specialized, taking the forty-quart cans of milk and putting the milk into a filter from which it went into a pasteurizer. After all the milk was processed, they had to clean and sterilize the filters and all the pipes. There was an adult in charge of the pasteurization. In order for the man to take a vacation, he had Bruce certified to pasteurize the milk. During the summer, refrigerated trucks from Boston would come to the school to take the milk because there weren't enough students to use it all. Bruce was temporarily in charge of the milk operation. It was responsible work and Bruce was proud of it. During vacations they paid him for his work, first at fifty cents an hour and then at seventy-five cents an hour as he became more skilled.

He loved the outdoors, camping and hunting, and his Biology course. He found comfort and solace in the outdoors and expressed it this way:

> *Mount Hermon had 1,500 acres of land… I enjoyed long walks in the woods or along the forested banks of the Connecticut River. One Sunday in early Spring, I sat beside the river from dawn until late afternoon, and watched the mighty Connecticut River's ice, which started as a sheet from one bank to the other, break up and float chunks of ice downstream. I love the hymns that we sang in our nondenominational chapel. I felt very much alone, and the chapel was very comforting.*

He spent hours in the woods and kept records of the fish in their lake. He became an excellent hunter and fisherman and began considering a career in conservation with the US Forest Service. Bruce liked the solitary life whether in books or in the wild. There was freedom there, both emotionally and physically. Perhaps the Forest Service would be a good choice for him.

He also learned a lot from his economics professor and wanted to try the stock market but didn't have enough money to even begin. Each student chose hypothetical stocks at the start of the term and, when they totaled current value at the end of the term, they had all profited. Bruce was very thrifty and Dad actually borrowed money from him at one point and then paid him back. He began buying stocks in 1952, the year he graduated from Mount Hermon, and continued to invest modestly for many years. When coupled with his frugal ways, these investments made him quite comfortable in his senior years. Bruce was a trooper. He didn't complain but looked for opportunities wherever they might occur.

Bob got a job through Choate working at an apple orchard in Connecticut. He said two men who worked there made homosexual advances towards him so he packed his bag and left on a train to Ohio. He then simply walked into the countryside looking for a job. We both had a strong desire to make our own way in the world. He found a job on a farm milking cows, feeding pigs, picking cherries and hoeing weeds. He felt good about his time there but Dad and Mom were concerned. Choate contacted them to report he had simply disappeared from his Connecticut job. They were beside themselves with worry. Bob did not contact them to let them know where he was or if he was all right. At harvest time he got hay fever and came home.

Bob had other summer jobs while we were in New Rochelle, including working in a bowling alley, an ice cream store, a Shell gas station and at the Westchester Airport where he managed to get flying lessons. But he was quick to take offense and lose his temper. In writing about this time he mentions how immoral or simply how wrong others were as his employers had been at the newspaper in Hong Kong. While on vacation in Florida a restaurant refused to serve him a drink because he was under the Florida drinking age of twenty-one. He caused such a ruckus he was asked to leave with his friends. He didn't respect rules or authority as much as he had as a youngster. He began to seem unable to back down or compromise, no matter the circumstances.

In the fall of 1952 Bob went on to Princeton, Bruce to Tufts and in 1953 I went to Dana Hall. Tenacre, the school I had attended three years earlier, was the junior school of Dana, so I adapted fairly easily there. I felt it was a finishing school where one learned to behave properly and received a smattering of education. However we had excellent teachers and my particular class had some bright and interesting students. There were also foreign students. And I could play on a different sports team each season. Field hockey was still my favorite sport, but I was also playing varsity basketball. I should have played tennis but, although I had excellent ground strokes from my practice on the New Rochelle High School courts, I had seldom served and never played matches. So I was too good for beginner tennis classes and not good enough for varsity play.

At Christmas time we had a carol sing in the main building which ended with *Silent Night*. We were young and full of energy; the air was crisp and as we came out of the main building to cross the street, we began singing *Jingle Bells* and dancing in a circle on the street. Evidently someone called the police because of the disturbance and the principal came out and ordered us to our dorms. She called a meeting of the student council and sent them around to the dorms to remind us of how ashamed we were to have caused a disturbance. I was not ashamed at all but resented how the administration had used the student council to do its work. I did not speak up. We were all aware our college admissions depended on teacher and school recommendations.

One of my favorite teachers was Mr. Smith in American History. My roommate, Aylin Kocibey, was Turkish and had

145

trouble remembering the difference between the Constitution and constipation with often hilarious results. One night before a test she asked for my help. I was quite good at determining what the teacher thought was important so I sat down with her and went over three possible subjects I thought might be on the test. And behold the next day it was one of them!

A few days later I received a request from Mr. Smith to come to his office. He straight out asked:

"Did you help Aylin cheat on the exam?"

"No. Why would you think that?"

He handed me her exam.

It read almost word for word like mine!

I explained to him the night before the exam she had asked me to help her and I had reviewed three questions which might be on the test. The question he had asked was one of them. She was smart enough to remember what I had said and repeat it on her test almost verbatim. Fortunately, he believed me.

Bruce had originally considered attending Colgate but felt he had not handled the interview well and was not accepted. He enrolled in Tufts University and it was a good fit. He majored in economics and accounting but also joined AFROTC (Air Force Reserve Officers Training Corps), thereby protecting himself from the draft for the Korean War. He received a modest stipend of $47.88 per month to bolster his finances. In the fall Dad paid him back the money he had borrowed and Bruce used it to buy his first stock. It might seem the discipline of the service would not be compatible with the sloppy boy he had been, but he took pride in his uniform and changed his ways. He wrote in his diary that he thought he would not live long as he would get killed in a war.

As Bruce became more aware of girls, he quickly found he did not want a society girl. Mom had arranged for him to escort Jean Miller to her coming out party in Rochester. He found the whole experience very intimidating. He was looking for a girl who liked the outdoors and could tolerate talk of the military and geopolitics. In October 1954, around Halloween, he joined a group of guys and gals who later became known as the Tufts Mountain Club. They took a trip up to a cabin in New Hampshire in an old hearse which they packed with mattresses for cushions and beer for dehydration. What a perfect time to drive up to an abandoned lead mine and gather hibernating bats! Bruce tells the story of what happened on their way back:

> *It was midnight, and the trip down the mountain was fun—college students in a hearse, drinking beer, and roaring down the mountain road, singing songs at the top of our lungs. We started around a tight mountain curve when I heard someone cry 'We're not going to make it!' The hearse hit the guard rail, and suddenly it was rolling over and over. The mattresses and human bodies cushioned us against the violence of the moment; suddenly everything stopped and there was a brief moment of silence.*
>
> *I opened the back door of the hearse and was startled to be looking down off the face of a cliff to a stream below. The back of the hearse was precariously perched out over the cliff, held up by two small trees that we had knocked down.*

They all climbed out through the driver's door. Fortunately, no one was seriously hurt. On the trip back to Tufts he met Margaret Canty, whom I call Midge. She was a student in physical therapy at Bouve College near Tufts, and was the date of one of the other boys in the van. Midge was Irish Catholic with bright red hair and real spirit. On another excursion with the Mountain Club, when they were coming back from a hunting trip, they were stopped by a policeman and a game warden who wanted to inspect the tag on the deer on top of their car. Bruce reported:

> *The policeman looked at the young men in the car—*
> *we were all very dirty from camping—and there was*
> *Midge, nice and clean, as usual.*
> *"Are you related to these men?" he asked.*
> *"I should hope not!" Midge replied.*

She had spunk. Bruce felt Catholics often had closed minds, but he was drawn to her. He commented in his diary "I have met a girl by the name of Midge Canty who is a truly wonderful girl; the only problem is that she is a Catholic." They had a few dates but were not very serious.

During the summer after his junior year Bruce went to AFROTC summer camp. The experience confirmed he was a very good marksman. Our family had used rifles in the past in Hong Kong and in Mendon, but not competitively. Bruce's eyesight was excellent and his aim steady. He had found another reason he liked the Air Force—it offered him an opportunity to excel. Like most of us, he enjoyed doing something he did well. He began thinking seriously of a career in the Air Force.

# X

Mom and Dad were very proud of Bob when he went to Princeton to become an engineer. This is what they envisioned for their older son. Unfortunately, things did not work out the way they anticipated. Mom hoped engineering would be the right occupation for Bob because he was not a natural reader like Bruce. His strengths seemed to be in mathematics and physics.

He continued flying lessons near the campus and soon soloed. He signed up for Air Force ROTC. The Air Force gave him a physical exam and found his eyesight was not keen enough to be a military pilot. He was disappointed, quit the AFROTC program, and switched from aeronautical to electrical engineering. The courses became more difficult as time passed. He did not feel confident in calculus or other mathematical subjects dealing with concepts he could not envision such as an infinite series. To him higher mathematics seemed vague and dishonest. The concept of the square root of minus one was used frequently, and it worked, but he sensed it was not logical. Did we only pretend we knew what we were doing?

Bob increasingly saw life as threatening. One Princeton tradition was the Freshman theft of the clapper from the bell tower while the Sophomore class defended it. A scuffle ensued between the two classes. Bob saw this confrontation as unrest on the campus while others saw it as Freshman hijinks.

Bob not only wanted a girlfriend, he felt he needed one. He met many girls in the social whirl of Princeton, but the

149

relationships didn't last. Although our mother made friends easily, I don't remember her specifically teaching us how to make friends. She had grown up with the same friends all her life, so what we faced was foreign to her until she was an adult and had already acquired those skills. We were all quite shy and used to being rejected. We needed to learn to listen to others and genuinely empathize with them as I had been trying to do since New Rochelle. Bob seemed to see girls as fulfilling his needs, but I don't think he spent much time asking himself how he could meet their needs. So they moved on.

Bob found the engineering program very demanding. He also found it very exciting because many new discoveries were being made and evaluated. One of his professors said we would soon be going to the moon. Dr. Einstein came to listen to one of the lectures Bob attended. The more difficult the classes became the more he doubted his ability. Yet he claims others found him arrogant. He seemed to combine self-righteousness and insecurity. He wanted to understand everything thoroughly—if he didn't, it could not be true. Two negatives couldn't make a positive even if the concept made certain things work. He expected to be able to prove and envision everything. What was an infinite number? It was like trying to define God. He saw life through a sharp moral camera, even mathematics.

While he was struggling with these deep concepts, his social life was frustrating. Two of his friends joined one club, but he joined another which seemed more intellectual. He admired Dad's academic accomplishments, particularly his knowledge of Latin. He wanted Dad to be proud of him but he was not strong in the same areas. He had trouble in English which may have been due to mild dyslexia. Somehow, I could admire my mother's style while seeing myself as an athlete and student and not as a failure because I wasn't clothes conscious or beautiful. Bob wanted to excel in his father's intellectual role but he was no more suited to it than I was to mother's style. He resented people telling him to go in a particular direction. He wanted to go his own way, but he didn't know what way it was.

In February 1955 Dad was transferred to Rochester where he returned to the export department of Kodak to edit a monthly trade paper. Our parents initially moved into the small cabin in Mendon and Dad drove off to work in Rochester every morning. Mom felt abandoned and lonely. There were few people within walking distance. One morning when the alarm clock rang Dad rolled out of bed and fell to the floor. His left side was paralyzed and his speech slurred. Mom now had a purpose and devoted herself to it. Within a few months Dad was back on his feet and at work, although he continued to have difficulty walking and talking.

Their enforced time together in the cabin helped him to realize Mom needed a project to keep her busy. Since he felt having her take a job was out of the question, he encouraged her to plan and build a proper house on the hill overlooking Irondequoit Creek. In fact, it gave them both something to do while he was recovering from the stroke. He also used the time to reevaluate his life as his career was sidetracked. His father, the last of his parents' generation, had died recently. Now they were the oldest generation, and they needed to think about their future.

In June I graduated cum laude from Dana Hall. Mom was in seventh heaven, not because of my academic achievement but because of the ceremonies of graduation. She loved the pomp and circumstance. We all wore white dresses and carried a single rose. The ceremony took place in the Wellesley Congregational Church on a spectacular day. I was concerned Dad might not be able to attend due to the remaining paralysis on his left side. With the help of Mom's brother Ray, who drove them from Rochester, he was there.

Mom said she wanted me to go to a southern school I considered insufficiently intellectual. I applied to Mount Holyoke and Harvard/Radcliffe. The bookstores in Cambridge fascinated me as did a three-two program with Harvard and M.I.T. Under this plan one could spend three years at Harvard and two years at M.I.T., graduating with a B.A. from Harvard and B.S. from M.I.T. Mount Holyoke appealed to me because my tennis friend went there, loved it, and invited me up for an enjoyable weekend. I was accepted at both and chose Harvard where I planned to major in aeronautical engineering (on the three/two program) or Chinese history. My father was proud of me but I didn't think Mom was. She was afraid a smart girl would scare off boys—and the goal of college was to catch a man, wasn't it? Later she said she wanted me to go to Harvard but knew kids my age liked to oppose their parents so by pushing another school she could guarantee I would want to go somewhere else. She knew I was not looking for a husband but perhaps, simply by exposure, I would find one. In fact, one of the things I liked about Harvard was not having to play dumb—these young men were at least as smart or smarter than I was.

Bob found a summer job working for General Electric as an engineer. He said he was asked to sign a form assigning anything he invented in his lifetime to GE. He felt betrayed and angry. I suspect he misunderstood the details of the assignment but he became angry so quickly he did not calmly look into the matter. He continued to work there because he needed the money but became convinced he should not be an engineer. Then he received a letter from Princeton informing him his grades were below the minimum needed for graduation with his class. He quit. Perhaps this was the same problem Mom had at the University of Rochester. He had become mentally disoriented; therefore he could not concentrate on his studies, therefore his grades fell, therefore he did not have enough credits to graduate with his class. Even today, Bob does not know exactly what the letter said. Could he have stayed in, possibly changed his major, and graduated a year later? Could he have taken a year off and then returned to finish? Was he expelled with no alternative? He was very upset and quit.

Bob felt he had been asked to leave because a Dean had seen him watching the Joe Sugar riot, a college melee, and thought he was a participant. If that were why he was leaving, many more students would have had to leave. As usual he saw his situation was unfair—life was always unfair. He did not seem to be of the same trooper mentality as Bruce or I were. He did complain about Mom pushing him, unfair teachers, lack of a steady girlfriend and many other things. Today, in my eighties, I am amazed at how many people complain about life being unfair. Where did they get the idea life is fair? He went back to Princeton to talk to AFROTC which he had quit earlier. They had nothing to offer him which "made him angry" (his words). He decided to join the Army in September just as Bruce was heading off to his last year at Tufts and I was starting Harvard.

The same summer Bob's life was collapsing, Bruce was finding his way. He attended AFROTC summer camp at Ethan Allen AFB in Vermont. It was a tough experience, both physically and mentally, but it gave him a strong sense of accomplishment. He had evidently found a career with a purpose in which he could be successful.

Bob has both good and bad things to say about his army experience. I think he enjoyed getting into good physical shape and his Army friendships. But his sense of rejection resurfaced again and again. Of course, I understood rejection because I had been experiencing it every time I changed schools and particularly in New Rochelle. The difference was I EXPECTED rejection, and he seemed consumed by its

153

unfairness. I did not like it but felt rejection was the result of simply being different—and we were always different.

He survived basic training in Fort Dix, New Jersey, although he complained about the cold and the lack of education of the non-commissioned officers. He went home for Christmas but his pride in being in good shape and surviving basic training was dissipated by his reception in Mendon. Veterans saw him as thoroughly green and his ex-girlfriends considered him a drop-out. He had little status with anyone. Even Mom and Dad were not proud of him, and he had always wanted their approval.

He was assigned to Fort Chaffee, Arkansas, to be trained as a forward observer in artillery school. The people in Arkansas were friendlier to soldiers than they had been up north. He soon moved on to Fort Knox, Kentucky. His duty there was pleasant, but he grew increasingly disturbed. He met one girl who liked him but her father prohibited her from going out with soldiers. He thought American soldiers should be admired but often they were not.

One night when he was on guard duty at Fort Knox, Kentucky, he removed the clip from his carbine, pointed it up in the air and fired. He did not realize he had a live round in the chamber. Now he felt he would really be in trouble, but there was nothing but silence. When guard duty was over and the men turned in their equipment, the sergeant reported to the lieutenant one live round was missing. Each man denied he had the missing round, including Bob. Now he couldn't even respect himself. He was not even good at being a soldier. Someone must have noticed his increasing agitation because the Captain called him into his office and discussed his personal life and goals. Bob felt he no longer had any goals and was at the edge of a precipice.

Then he was posted to Indiantown Gap, Pennsylvania, for the summer. It was a National Guard training camp. There were few men regularly stationed there, and he spent a good deal of time exploring the surrounding mountainous terrain. He easily fell into arguments with the other men whether over poker or fossils—it didn't seem to matter. One long weekend he went to Mendon. He did not feel welcome there, either by his parents or his girlfriends. One morning he just started crying, much as Mom had in 1944 in San Francisco. At the end of the weekend he returned to Indiantown Gap. Bob described what happened next:

> I just walked away. I walked down a hill to an empty building to think. I could not go on any more the way I was living. It was intolerable. My heart was beating fast. I walked into the mountains. The wildlife was there. I saw deer and pheasants. Some military police came to me and asked me what I was doing. I explained to them I was just taking a walk. They went on. I went to a store along the country road and bought some candy. I did not have much money. I walked back into the woods to think. What could I do? I tried to think rationally, but there were no answers. As night came I went to an abandoned barracks and tried to make a bed for myself out of newspapers. The cold night was getting to me and I was shivering. I did not have a coat. I felt isolation. And anger and depression. I did not fit in anywhere or belong anywhere. Was I losing my mind? My heart was pounding. I was hungry. I thought of King David in the Old Testament who lost his mind. I began to understand how David must have felt. I tried to write a note, but my hands shook. So I gave up trying to sleep, and I walked. I heard some voices. It was a house and a family talking. They seemed to live in a different world than me. I picked a wildflower and put it in their mailbox. It was like saying

*goodbye. I continued to walk around at night. I was cold. I could see the stars. The stars seemed a sign of permanence and direction. Everything seemed insecure and changing. I began to cry. Somebody shined a flashlight into my face. There were several men asking me questions. I just cried. Someone put a coat over my shoulders. The military police gave me some water to drink and some pills and took me for a long ride.*

When he awoke, Bob found himself in the US Army hospital in Valley Forge, Pennsylvania. He had not been AWOL (absent without leave) because he had never left the military base nor had he disobeyed a direct order or done anything violent or criminal. He needed mental care and received it. In August 1956 he was given an honorable discharge and headed home. But where was home? Our parents were in Mendon so he went there. For us, home had to be where our immediate family was. Our family was moving in different directions. In his own notes Bob wrote he was "free at last." Free from what? Expectations?

While Bob was struggling with his army experience, I was thoroughly enjoying my first year in college. I loved Harvard from the minute I arrived. It was my fourteenth, and last, school change. I could barely choose among the many great courses. I took one in Chinese history the students nicknamed *Rice Paddies* and a physics course to help me choose between possible majors. I also chose one in anthropology with a marvelous professor and one in architecture which opened my eyes to new vistas.

I signed up for Spanish III because I had loved Spanish at Dana Hall. The first day in my Spanish class upset me—it appeared the class stressed translating and grammar. I wanted to speak and read Spanish. Instead the professor asked us to translate phrases such as "I should have been swimming".

The next session the teacher announced that Spanish IV had only three students and, if anyone would like to make a change, it was in Room 302. I grabbed my books and fled up the stairs. Spanish IV was exactly what I wanted—reading and discussing classic Spanish short stories in Spanish—no translation. I would have flunked Spanish III, but I received a good grade in Spanish IV.

The social life was fun too. We had mixers with the Harvard boys and I met John Doede, whom I dated for several months. We drove down to Columbia University one Saturday to see the Harvard/Columbia football game. It was a cloudy day, and the wind began to howl. A hurricane was coming, so we left the game early and headed back to Cambridge. As we drove north, the weather became rapidly worse, and it turned dark. The main highways closed due to flooding and soon we were lost on back roads. We pulled into a Dairy Queen on top of a hill where we would probably be dry. Everything, including the Dairy Queen, had closed. John called his parents from the outdoor pay phone there, giving them its telephone number. His parents contacted the police who said to stay where we were until morning—there was flooding all around us.

There were four of us in the station wagon. We spread out as best we could and tried to sleep. At dawn we started off again. Connecticut was under martial law. The Connecticut River was roaring and tearing down houses on its banks. There were military amphibious vehicles where we tried to cross the river and only one lane was open on the remaining bridge. We made it across but were told the bridge collapsed later that day. John's parents lived in Connecticut so we headed to his house. They were anxiously awaiting us and insisted we all call our parents immediately.

Mom answered the phone

Me: "It's OK Mom. We are safe in Connecticut at John's parents' home."

Mom: "Why shouldn't you be?"

Me: "There has been a big hurricane and Connecticut is under martial law. But we are fine."

Mom was calm and had obviously not listened to the news.

After some hot food and warm showers we headed on to Harvard. When I entered the dorm, everyone shouted at once.

"Call your mom!"

After I had called her from Connecticut she had turned on the news and THEN panicked.

At Christmastime Mom wanted me to come out at a cotillion in Rochester. Cotillions were formal balls in which young ladies were introduced to society. I was not interested, but it meant a lot to her so I agreed. John Doede was my escort. Living in Connecticut he was more familiar with them than I was. Mother and I were different people, and I was beginning to find myself. I loved academics and sports but she admired clothes, wealth and social standing. She was not a snob nor a bigot. In new communities, she always quickly made friends with taxi drivers and anyone else who really knew the town. I think she loved the social life she had seen at a distance as a young girl in Rochester and wanted it for herself and her children. It would not cost me much to oblige her. She was so happy the night of the cotillion she cried, this time from happiness. After Mom's death Dad told me she had sold her diamond engagement ring to pay for the party and replaced it with a cubic zirconia ring. Typically, I hadn't noticed.

At Harvard I became more outgoing. I think it had something to do with Mom's strong personality. When she was around, I was simply in her shadow. When she wasn't there, I became more like her. I was elected social chairman of my dorm, something Mom could not fathom because she did not know the different person I became when she was not there.

I plowed into academics and sports at Harvard. I loved the classes and had some excellent, challenging professors.

My physics course was interesting, and I did so well I was chosen for a special laboratory group. One experiment we did made a big impact on me. My results did not agree with established predictions, probably because I had made a simple mathematical mistake or an inaccurate measurement. I felt the professor wanted me to make my results conform to the theory. He literally said, "How can someone who is so smart be so dumb!" I was crestfallen because I loved physics and hoped to major in aeronautical engineering. I did not have much self-confidence and bowed to his criticism. I must not be smart enough to major in physics. He should have told me to go ahead with my data and develop another test to support them. Then I would have found my answers wrong and learned to go over my results more carefully the next time.

I finished the course with a good grade but went no further with physics although to this day I follow new discoveries in the discipline from continued interest. Today many women tell stories of how they left the sciences due to little support from their professors. It wasn't all his fault-I should have had more backbone. How could I have so much resilience on the athletic field and cave in so easily to a Harvard professor?

In Chinese studies I had another experience which reflected the same problem. I discussed an issue with Professor Fairbanks, whom my father greatly admired, about a historical event. He said, "Well, things tend to stay the same, don't they?" I mumbled something although I did not agree with him. Why couldn't I rise to the occasion and dispute the issue? Harvard professors obviously had to know more than I did—or did they? Thinking back, I believe Fairbanks was prodding me to stand up for a different opinion but I was too unsure of myself to even consider the possibility.

On the sports field, life was wonderful. I played three varsity sports, field hockey, basketball and fencing, and loved all of them. One fencing match exposed how differently I reacted to sports problems vs. Harvard professors.

We were fencing against Bouve College, which had undergraduates planning to be physical education teachers. My opponent was obviously new to the sport. She was very short and crouched down and stabbed me from below, a totally unorthodox move. She quickly amassed three points. I asked the umpire what would happen if I stepped off the mat. She did not know so I immediately stepped off the mat. The umpire went to find out what to do. I took the time to figure out that, because I was taller, my arms would be longer than my opponent's. When the umpire returned I stepped back on the mat. The next time my opponent lunged, I simply sucked in my gut and stabbed her from above. I quickly won the match. Why was I a tough athletic opponent but soft when questioned by Harvard professors?

I gradually began to gain confidence and argue contrasting positions. In my architecture class one assignment was to visit a local house under construction and, in our exam, describe what we liked and disliked about it. By mistake I had visited the home next door before realizing my error and reviewing the assigned building. In the exam, I briefly described my reaction to the assigned building and then said I thought the adjoining building was better and why. I got an A. I found Harvard professors welcomed push-back. I had spent years learning to give back to teachers what they wanted. Now I was experiencing professors who wanted you to engage and question.

Funding for girls' sports was limited (this was before Title IX), so our teams only traveled to a few away games at other colleges. These were called intercollegiate matches rather than varsity games although, years later, Harvard recognized them as varsity games and I was admitted to the Harvard Varsity Club. We even went to Wellesley once for an all New

England field hockey meet. At the end of my junior year I won the Senior Athletic Award for being on more varsity teams during my college career than any other female student even though I was a Junior. It was a white blazer with the Radcliffe/Harvard emblem on it. My daughters later both used it occasionally when they were in college. It is so unique the Harvard Athletic Department asked me to donate it to their archives if my family no longer wants it.

One day we had a varsity match against Pembroke/Brown but it ran late because of heavy traffic driving up from Rhode Island. A men's practice session was scheduled on the same court following our match. When our allotted time was up, the boys said the court was now theirs. We protested we were playing an intercollegiate match, and they had a practice session. Too bad. They pushed us off the court. If the same thing were to happen to me today, they would have to carry me off the court and would not hear the end of it. The Women's Rights movement was in the future.

# XI

In the spring of 1956 I was studying in the dorm one evening when one of my friends shouted down the hall, "Anyone want to quit studying and go out for a drink?" She had a Harvard Law School friend who was looking to double date. I was happy to take a break. We went out to a local bar nearby, and the guys ordered drinks for all four. They had been through college and the service so were obviously old enough to legally drink. No one questioned us. I felt very grown-up. My date was Tom Bain and I liked him.

The next week Tom called and asked for another date. I already had a date and had been taught never to cancel one engagement because I preferred another, so I said I was otherwise engaged. He requested the name of another friend so I set him up with a classmate from Fargo, North Dakota. Then I spent a miserable week making no commitments and waiting to see whether he would ask me out again or call my friend. Eventually he called, but it was the end of the term so we only had one other date in the spring. Would he contact me again in the fall?

Bruce graduated from Tufts in June and was commissioned a Second Lieutenant in the US Air Force Reserve. He expected to be called up to duty shortly so he took a temporary job as a waiter at a resort in Maine while he waited. Midge, who was studying to be a physical therapist, had a summer job at an Easter Seal camp for handicapped children further north. She still had another year to go at Bouve. Dad had a theory that men fall in love when they are ready and Bruce feels this was when he fell in love with Midge. He was ready for his career and a serious relationship. He made several long trips north to spend time with Midge. But first there was his service commitment.

In August he headed south to Lackland AFB in Texas. On the way he stopped in Mendon. We were all there for what I consider one of the most difficult moments in our lives as a family. Bob had just returned from the army hospital with his discharge. Mom and Dad suggested he go down to Texas with Bruce to find a job. It went something like this:

Bob: I need a place to stay while I get on my feet.

Parents: You can stay almost anywhere, so go to Texas with Bruce and get started. There are many jobs open there in the oil fields.

Bob: How can you send me away when I need you the most?

Parents: We would be doing so for your own good.

Bob: I won't go. I need to be here, get a job, graduate from college and develop a home—which I have never had.

It ended bitterly. I stayed in my room, consoled by my cat as usual, listening but not participating. Bob eventually left the house and went to the cabin. Bruce drove off alone the next morning for Texas.

Bob was so absorbed in his own problems he did not appreciate Mom and Dad had serious problems of their own. Dad's career was stalled, he was recovering from a stroke, and Mom continued to have serious headaches. She took lots of pills, but they did not seem to help. We never had a definitive explanation of the headaches although as early as Hawaii they were blamed on allergies and later on depression. I never heard the word migraine applied to them. Whatever the cause, they could be debilitating.

Living in the country, instead of calming her, isolated her from the social life she so much needed. Dad wanted to protect her and now a full-grown son, who should be self-sufficient, was causing additional stress and asking them for help. Bob should go with Bruce to Texas, find a job and support himself. They had been supporting him for years—now they needed to support each other. The problem appeared differently from Bob's point of view than it did from Mom and Dad's.

Bob stayed on in the cabin at Mendon. I had a summer job at a local department store in Rochester. One day when I came home from work I couldn't find my cat. It turned out Bob had shot and killed it. He said he had an allergy to cats, so he got rid of the problem. I felt there could have been other solutions. We had had cats and dogs in our homes for years. It was August and his allergy was probably due to hay fever, which he knew he had, rather than to my cat. I thought he was just so consumed by anger, resentment and frustration he took it out on his successful sister of whom he was now probably jealous. How had he gone from being the family leader to this stage of despair? He might even be dangerous to himself and others.

I escaped by going off to my second year at Harvard. It was an exciting time for me. My Chinese courses were going splendidly, and I was making lots of important contacts in the field. When I expressed an interest in going back to China, my advisor, Professor Schwartz, recommended I contact Professor Brown across the Charles River at Boston University as he was organizing an academic visit there. I called Dr. Brown, and we met at a Chinese restaurant in Cambridge. He introduced me to a friend who joined us. We had a fascinating luncheon talking about the trip. China was then closed to tourists so this would be a unique academic opportunity. At the end of the meal Professor Brown turned to his friend and said:

"Shall we tell her the truth?"

Friend: "I don't know the truth."

Me: "What are you talking about?"

It turned out the two men had been in graduate school together and Brown had pulled an intricate practical joke on his friend. Brown thought this whole meeting was the retaliation for his previous scheme. Brown apologized to me for the deception and paid for lunch. I was quite disappointed.

In the fall I had a few more dates with Tom Bain but I was also dating Bo, a young assistant professor of metallurgy at MIT. I liked them both, and they both knew I was dating other people. Things became complicated. I was still young and not thinking about marriage, but they were about seven years older and ready for a new phase in their lives. In the spring I had a date with Bo to go sailing on the Charles River. He arrived at the dorm to pick me up when I saw Tom walking up the pathway outside. I asked my roommates to take Bo upstairs while I went down and told Tom I couldn't see him because I had a date with Bo. He said nothing and went away.

It was a lovely day for sailing and Bo was good company, but I couldn't stop thinking about Tom. Several days went by and Tom didn't call. I was a nervous wreck; in fact, so disoriented the cook in our dorm briefly expelled me from helping in the kitchen due to carelessness. I don't know what I did, but I guess my lack of focus was the point. It had become clear. Tom was the one for me. Eventually (probably a couple of days but it seemed much longer) he did call and our courtship resumed. The biggest stumbling block for me was his assumption we would move to Sussex County, New Jersey, and live there the rest of our lives. Bo was an Assistant Professor at M.I.T. whose father had been a naval officer, and he planned to travel widely for conferences and for pleasure. Could I settle down in one place?

We try not to repeat our parents' mistakes and I felt Mom married a man whom she thought would give her travel and a family. She had certainly traveled and had a family, but the experience had been extremely stressful. I don't think she realized how much she wanted a social life. Like her Aunt Matie, she wanted to have FUN but most of the time, except for the early years in her marriage when they had servants and few responsibilities, it wasn't. I wanted to be sure I knew why I was marrying Tom and not look back and feel my life had been a failure. Now I'm not sure I knew what I wanted any more than my mother did. In choosing Tom was I actually seeking the stability I never had as a child?

Tom graduated from Harvard Law School in June 1958, a year before I was scheduled to graduate from Harvard. I never considered not finishing my degree, and he never brought up the subject. I accelerated so we could marry in January 1959, but I had to tackle a heavy course load. My grades were good, so I decided to try out for honors by writing a thesis. During Christmas vacation of 1957 I saw the very wedding dress I wanted on sale and decided to buy it. Mom was skeptical. What if things did not work out? We bought the dress.

Midge was at our house for Christmas as her relationship with Bruce was solidifying. My parents were happy with my choice of Tom, but Mom was not comfortable with Bruce's choice of Midge. First of all, she was Catholic and intended to remain so. Mom had herself been in love with a Catholic, Wink, when she was in high school, so I am surprised this bothered her so much. In addition, Midge was not of the social background to which Mom aspired. Frankly, I think this had more to do with her objection than religion did. Whichever it was, she took Midge aside and told her she did not feel Midge was the right girl for Bruce and she should end the relationship. Midge did not and she did not even tell Bruce what Mom had said.

Midge also received opposition from her Boston relatives. They felt her decision to major in physical therapy was akin to deciding to be a sumo wrestler. There was a strong push for her to enter a convent and become a nun. Some family members were trying to set her up with dates "with the right kind of boy." Midge herself had decided she wanted to leave Boston and find her own life. Bruce would certainly not be living in Boston.

By attending summer school and taking extra courses during the regular school year, I would have enough credits to finish all my course work before my marriage. With my added classes my athletic activity had to diminish. I attended Harvard Summer School to earn more credits. It did not appear that a degree in Far Eastern History would lead to a job in Sussex County, New Jersey, so I took two courses in the Harvard Graduate School of Education. Perhaps I could find a teaching job. I was so exhausted during my last exam my hands were shaking and I could barely write. I started my thesis with Professor Schwartz in the fall but would need to finish it after I left Harvard.

Bruce and Midge's courtship was now proceeding by mail. The major stumbling block for them was the religious difference. Midge was a firm Catholic and wanted to be married in the church. She talked to me one day about their problem. Although young, I knew enough to step back and let them come to their own conclusions on this issue and their future together. I expressed no opinion.

In the spring of 1958 Midge flew down to Laredo, Texas, where Bruce was in flight school. When Bob left the army, he had noted he was "free at last." For Bruce, freedom meant the freedom of the outdoors and the skies. He knew Midge enjoyed camping and the outdoor life—she was a real trooper—but he was now committed to the Air Force and she needed to be comfortable with his choice. After several days together, and with Midge seeing more of Air Force life, they took a side trip to Nuevo Laredo in Mexico. He proposed and was immediately accepted, but they kept the engagement secret for a while.

In June, Bruce moved on to Moody Air Force Base in Georgia where he took a course in Catholicism required for non-Catholics marrying a Catholic. He had to sign a paper saying he would not interfere in the religion of his wife or his children, and he did so comfortably because he felt he was not saying his family would necessarily be Catholic but that he would let them choose for themselves. Now the problem became finding a priest who would marry them in the Boston area, an assignment easier said than done.

Shortly after moving in to the cabin in Mendon, Bob began working for the Rochester Telephone Company. He also enrolled part-time in the University of Rochester, transferring what courses he could from Princeton. His goal was to receive a Bachelor of Science degree by taking one course per semester. He started to rebuild his self-confidence both with responsibilities in his job and in the courses he took at the University of Rochester. He wanted a home and felt he needed not just a girlfriend, but a wife. His dating became very serious. and he became engaged to a girl who worked at the telephone company, but they broke up as they realized how many differences there were between them. He dated a few of my friends, Jane Searjeant, Jean Miller, Audrey Salyer and the riding teacher, Olga Walters, at a nearby ranch where I took a few lessons.

Bob drove me over to my first riding lesson. Olga showed me how to mount the horse. I had ridden a little at a dude ranch when I was much shorter and remembered how hard it was to get up on the saddle. With all my sports activity I was in great shape and much taller now. When I tried to mount, I jumped so high I went sailing over the horse's back, reaching for its mane as I realized my mistake. I ended up on the ground hanging underneath his neck. Bob, standing along the rail watching, burst into laughter. Olga shot him a nasty look—it was hilarious, but he shouldn't laugh at her student.

It delighted Mom to learn her cousin Audie's daughter Marny was planning to come to Canada to marry her boyfriend Tony Howe. Audie had been Mom's substitute when she had given up her job escorting the Japanese ambassador's son back to Japan. Marny came to Mendon and stayed with Mom and Dad. Tony arrived and moved into the cabin with Bob. Marny and Tony married in the Mendon Presbyterian Church in February 1958, with Bob as best man and Dad walking Marny down the aisle. The reception was at the big house in Mendon and then they were off to Toronto where Tony had a job.

Bob took a long vacation trip to Colorado and California and thought about his future. When he came back, he asked Olga Walter to marry him and she accepted. In September they married in the home of Olga's friend Peggy Neale. Bob had refused to be married in a Catholic church, as Olga's parents had requested, so they did not attend the wedding, but Mom and Dad did.

Bruce and Midge planned to marry in her father's church in Boston because she would leave the area for good when he was posted to various airbases. The problem was her local priest would not marry her to a non-Catholic. Midge's father had been a high school friend of the eminent Richard Cushing, later Cardinal Cushing, and her father told her priest he would contact Father Cushing if the matter could not be overcome. It was.

Then another problem surfaced. Bruce's baptismal record was destroyed when Manila was bombed in World War II. If he weren't baptized, he wasn't a Christian. Fortunately we had a black-and-white photo of Mom and Bob in the Philippines with a blond baby all dressed up. On the back was the identification *Millie and Sonny at Bruce's baptism*. At this point the local priest was so relieved he set the wedding date of November 22nd. There was a possibility Mom wouldn't come because of her opposition to Catholicism, but she did. This time it was Olga who would not come because Midge was having the Catholic service Olga and her parents had wanted. Typically Bruce had shown more flexibility than Bob. Mom gave Midge the nickname Candy because of her red hair and a misunderstanding of her last name, Canty. The honeymoon was a long drive to Geiger Air Force Base in Spokane, Washington, to his next assignment.

Tom and I had been the first planning our marriage and were the last married. On January 31st, 1959, I married Tom Bain. I took my last exams at Harvard during January and then rushed home for the wedding. Everything had to happen in three days because my bridesmaids had to get back to Harvard for their next term. Mom was in heaven. Our house was brimming with my bridesmaids and the cabin with the ushers. My parents moved out to a motel for the weekend so we could have the space and they could have peace and quiet. After the wedding at the Third Presbyterian Church in Rochester and the reception across the street at the Century Club, we headed off to Canada for our honeymoon (all we could afford) and Dad and Mom we left alone to adjust to the empty house.

Within one year we were all married and started on our new adventures. Moving constantly is stressful but a psychologist once told my mother it either makes you or breaks you. Dad soldiered on but had to deal with the physical consequences of stress, including a heart attack and stroke. In several instances he did not have his family to support him because he had made the wise decision to send them to safety. Mom suffered from headaches for years which eventually led to her having shock treatments. She tried to be a trooper and keep a happy face but inside she was suffering. Bob's path was similar to Mom's with some academic failure and depression. He divorced three times but became more stable later in life and finally found a home in Colorado. Bruce was probably the best adjusted of us all—he found his own way and stuck to it. I am constantly amazed at how fortunate I have been. My immediate family is my greatest blessing. I do not lack for food and shelter, things almost everyone around me takes for granted but I do not, and every day I wake up and look out a picture window at our peaceful farm. People often comment I don't seem to be afraid to do anything—what a change from the fearful child. At eighty-one years of age, I am still almost hyperactive, running from one activity to another and charging the net.

We have each found our own way to a meaningful life, but the voyage was not easy. I did not expect it to be either easy or fair.

# epilogue

After Dad's retirement our parents continued to travel, to Russia, around the world again, and back to the Philippines with the Executive Service Corps. While living in Green Valley south of Tucson, Arizona, Mom went blind. She died in Green Valley at age 70 after giving Dad a list of ten women she thought might make good second wives. He visited Eleanor Breed and proposed marriage but Eleanor was about to depart on a trip of her own around the world with her sister Clara. Eleanor and Dad married the following year. They moved to a retirement community in San Diego where Eleanor's sister Clara had settled. Dad died there at 85, then Eleanor and finally Clara.

Bob and Olga had a son Scotty who died in a farm accident. Bob moved to Colorado, and he and Olga divorced. He graduated from Denver Law School and married Jean Miller. They had two children, Paul and Pam, and divorced. He married a third time for a brief period with no children. He now lives alone in Lakewood, Colorado.

Bruce had a successful career as a fighter pilot winning the Distinguished Flying Cross and leaving the service as a Major. He then took private employment including working in Saudi Arabia and Georgia. He survived kidnapping, drowning, poisoning and was reported missing over the Pacific while in the Air Force. Midge worked as a physical therapist as they moved around to different air force bases. They had three children, Julie, Brian and Jean, and now live in Kentucky.

Bruce and Midge are valued members of their community, volunteering particularly with Hispanic immigrants.

Tom and I stayed on his family's farm in New Jersey. We had three children, Carolyn, Virginia and Gordon. He was a successful small-town lawyer and judge. I continued to travel for pleasure but never moved off the farm. I have had an enjoyable career as a tennis professional and as a volunteer in my community. He passed away in 2016 and I was able to find the time to write this book.